STUDIES IN HISTORY, ECONOMICS AND
PUBLIC LAW

Edited by the

FACULTY OF POLITICAL SCIENCE
OF COLUMBIA UNIVERSITY

———

NUMBER 544

THE EMANCIPATION
OF THE AUSTRIAN PEASANT
1740-1798

BY

EDITH MURR LINK

THE EMANCIPATION
OF THE
AUSTRIAN PEASANT
1740-1798

BY

EDITH MURR LINK

OCTAGON BOOKS

A DIVISION OF FARRAR, STRAUS AND GIROUX

New York   1974

Reprinted 1974

by special arrangement with Columbia University Press

OCTAGON BOOKS

A DIVISION OF FARRAR, STRAUS & GIROUX, INC.

19 Union Square West

New York, N. Y. 10003

Library of Congress Cataloging in Publication Data

Link, Edith Murr, 1923-
The emancipation of the Austrian peasant, 1740-1798.

Reprint of the ed. published by Columbia University Press, New
York, which was issued as no. 544 of Columbia University. Faculty of Political Science. Studies in history, economics and public
law.

Originally presented as the author's thesis, Columbia, 1949.

Bibliography: p.
1. Peasantry—Austria.   2. Land tenure—Austria.   3. Serfdom
—Austria.   I. Title.   II. Series: Columbia studies in the social
sciences, no. 544.

HD634.L5   1974   323.3   74-4264
ISBN 0-374-95017-2

Printed in USA by
Thomson-Shore, Inc.
Dexter, Michigan

To

Alfred and Adele Murr

PREFACE

An exclusive landowner-peasant relationship, in which the state had little interest and less influence, was the basis of the rural constitution of eighteenth-century Austria before the accession of Maria Theresa. A little over a century later the Austrian peasant was no longer the subject of a lord but a citizen of the state. The factors which made for the transformation were many and varied: mercantilism, fiscalism, the Enlightenment, liberalism. The purpose of the present study is to investigate why the central government interfered with the landowner-peasant relationship and how this interference ultimately led to the final emancipation of 1848. The provinces selected for the investigation corresponded roughly to those composing pre-1938 Austria: Upper and Lower Austria, Styria, Carinthia, Carniola, Tyrol and Vorarlberg. They were chosen partly because studies on the emancipation of the peasants existed for most of the non-German provinces of the Habsburg Empire, but principally because German Austria was thought to be an important link between the agrarian conditions in these provinces and those of Germany proper, partaking of the characteristics of both. The period which the study covers was designated by the events themselves. Seventeen forty, the accession of Maria Theresa, formed the logical beginning; seventeen ninety-eight, the year in which the state abandoned the role of protector of the peasants which it had played for half a century, an equally logical conclusion.

The author would like to thank President Charles W. Cole of Amherst College, under whose guidance this study was begun, Professor Carlton J. H. Hayes, who supervised the writing of the first draft, and Professor John H. Wuorinen, who kindly saw it through to completion, for their help and encouragement. Thanks are also due to Professors Shepard B. Clough, Geoffrey Bruun, and Garrett Mattingly who read the manuscript and offered valuable suggestions. The kindness of Professor Beatrice F. Hyslop of Hunter College helped through many a difficult hour. To Robert G. Link the author owes an intellectual as well as a personal debt.

EDITH MURR LINK

NEW YORK CITY, JULY 1948.

TABLE OF CONTENTS

CHAPTER IV

CHAPTER V

CHAPTER I

THE POSITION OF THE PEASANTRY AT THE ACCESSION OF MARIA THERESA

INTRODUCTION

THE roar of guns, the shouts of warriors, the humors of kings, the beauty of queens, the decorous smiles of diplomats have for centuries dominated the minds of those who have written the history of Western Europe. But beneath the roars and the smiles there is, for those who care to look, another story. It is the story of those who manned the armies of conquest, who provided the funds which allowed kings to have humors and queens to be beautiful, and who, by the smiles of diplomats, might easily be changed from citizens of one country to subjects of another. How they lived their lives or died their deaths is largely unknown to us. They performed no great deeds, and only as a faceless multitude did they leave an imprint on history. Yet the peasants formed for many ages the overwhelming majority of the population of Europe.

Few have cared to study their history, and those who have studied it frequently found themselves enmeshed in difficulties. Having as a source only the written word of their ancestors they have been forced to realize that those who could write had little interest in recording the story, while those who knew and understood it best were rarely able to write.

Indeed our knowledge of the peasantry seems to be confined largely to those periods when, driven by misery and starvation, they intruded into the dynastic quarrels and religious arguments of the political world. Such intrusions were rarely tolerated. John Ball, Wat Tyler, Thomas Muenzer, the *croquants* and Barefeet of the France of Richelieu, the rebellious serfs of seventeenth-century Bohemia shared the same fate. Almost invariably greater suppression, higher dues, longer hours of work followed these rebellions: they provided the feudal lords with a plausible excuse to break their previous agreements with the peasants.

Only during the last decades of the eighteenth century and the first half of the nineteenth did the literate world take any particular interest in peasant conditions and problems, an interest which had no sooner arisen than it was superseded by the attention which had to be given to the already powerful bourgeoisie and the rising industrial proletariat. Yet in these few decades the peasants had profited tremendously. Between 1780 and 1850 centuries of serfdom, bondage and subjection were dissolved.

In German Austria, as in all the lands of the Habsburg monarchy, the process was a long and tedious one. It began with the accession of Maria Theresa, but only the aftermath of the Revolution of 1848 brought its final fulfillment. It is not the length of time it took, however, which is particularly notable in the transformation of the Austrian peasant from the subject of the feudal lord to the citizen of the state, but rather the manner in which it was first attempted.

In most European countries the battle between the attempts at centralization of the state and the decentralizing tendency of the nobility had been fought long before the justice of the manorial relationship had been called into question. In the Austrian hereditary lands, however, the unifying tendency of the state came late, and when it did come all the other problems of eighteenth-century Europe, the question of the Rights of Man, the abolition of feudalism, anti-clericalism and even the beginnings of nineteenth-century nationalism became involved in it.

How far these problems had to become part of the situation, or how far they were injected into it by the social conscience and the somewhat doctrinaire philosophy of Joseph II, we shall discuss later. It must be remembered, however, that the policy of state intervention in manorial affairs was inaugurated, not by the "Revolutionary Emperor," but by his vastly more conservative predecessor, the Empress Maria Theresa.

Up to the accession of Maria Theresa the traditional alliance between the ruling house and the nobility with regard to the peasantry was virtually unbroken. Both had opposed with equal vigor the peasantry's demands in the great Peasants' War of 1525-6,[1] while the rebellion of 1595 was crushed by the combined forces of Archduke Matthias and an army of mercenaries hired by the estates and led by Gotthardt von Starhemberg. It is significant that although the revolt was largely of a religious character, as much concerned with the abolition of the mass and the installation of Protestant ministers as with the reduction of the peasants' dues and services, Starhemberg, himself a zealous and devout Protestant, headed the forces of law and order. He is said to have hanged Protestants and Catholics with impartiality.[2]

In the last major uprising among the German Austrian peasantry during the Thirty Years' War, the crown and nobility again joined hands to crush the insurgents. This time they crushed the rebellion with such ferocity and treachery [3] that one can hardly wonder at the dull resignation with which the Austrian peasantry subsequently bore its fate.

In its efforts to emancipate itself, the peasantry had been completely and decisively defeated. It had been beaten on social

[1] For the history of the Peasants' War as it affected Austria see: Walter Honold, *Die Meraner Artikel*, Tuebingen, 1936, pp. 53 and 62-66; Johannes Janssen, *Geschichte des Deutschen Volkes*, Freiburg, 1897, II, 482; A. Bebel, *Der Deutsche Bauernkrieg*, Braunschweig, 1876, pp. 213-23; Friedrich Engels, *Der Deutsche Bauernkrieg*, Berlin, 1908, p. 113; F. M. Mayer and Hans Pirchegger, *Geschichte und Kulturleben Deutschoesterreichs*, Vienna, 1931, p. 8; E Belfort Bax, *The Peasants' War in Germany*, London, 1899, pp. 326-28; Günther Franz, *Der Deutsche Bauernkrieg*, Berlin, 1933, pp. 254-94.

[2] Albin Czerny, *Der Zweite Bauernaufstand in Oberoesterreich*, Linz, 1890, pp. 12 ff.

[3] Albin Czerny, *Bilder aus der Zeit der Bauernunruhen*, Linz, 1876; also F. M. Mayer and H. Pirchegger, *op. cit.*, pp. 104-105.

issues in 1525, on social and religious issues in 1595, and on the religious question in 1626. From then on it fought no more. First by compulsion, then by habit, it accepted the authorities which providence seemed to have placed over it. But its conquerors could not agree among themselves. It was from their conflict that the changes in the fate of the peasantry were to come.

THE POSITION OF THE PEASANTS IN 1740

The peasant's relationship with his lord was of course much closer and more immediate than that with the Emperor. Indeed, up to 1740, except in times of extraordinary stress such as the peasant revolts, he would probably have no contact with the Imperial government at all. Economically, politically, administratively and legally, the noble was his master. Except for a few freeholders (*Freisassen*), whose number was always insignificant, the country was divided into thousands of domains (*Herrschaften*) [4] in which the lord performed all the functions of a sovereign. As a rule there were several villages in such a district, communities which in the main governed themselves, subject only to " custom, privileges, and the provincial constitution." [5] Excessively large domains, the " kingdoms " within the kingdom that existed in the Slav provinces, were on the whole rare in German Austria, but were, to mention only the Diedrichstein possessions in Styria, not unknown. Many lords owned more than one estate; in some cases they possessed as many as twenty or more, three to four being quite usual among the higher nobility. Since in such instances the lord of the manor would frequently be unwilling or unable to supervise his holdings personally, the custom of hiring members of the lower nobility to do the job grew up. Besides these, there were lord's officials of various

4 That is, as far as the rural population was concerned. There existed of course a number of free cities, subject only to the Emperor.

5 Ignaz Beidtel, *Geschichte der Oesterreichischen Staatsverwaltung*, Innsbruck, 1889, p. 4.

kinds—bookkeepers, supervisors, hunters and a general fac-
totum called *Wirtschaftsbeamter*. Through these men, the
nobles exercised the rights which, by the provincial constitu-
tions and in the absence of a strong central government, were
so generously granted to them.

As landowners they allocated fields to the peasants. Depend-
ing on whether land was located within the village community
or on the lord's demesne, the fields were called rustic (*rustikal*)
or domestic (*domestikal*), a distinction which was to become
important for purposes of taxation. Both rustic and domestic
fields could either be bought by the peasant or held in usufruct
only. But even where a purchase had taken place, the lord
retained the overlordship (*Obereigentum*) and reversionary
right (*Heimfallsrecht*), while, where the peasants were tenants only, their right to occupy land tended to be limited in
time. In Carinthia, for instance, tenancy was as a rule restricted to what was then picturesquely called two bodies
(*zwei Leiber*), meaning two generations.[6]

No matter on what terms the peasant held his land he
could not sell, mortgage or divide it without the permission
of the lord; on the other hand, the nobles claimed for themselves the right to convert peasant land into noble land and
vice versa, a custom which had grown particularly prevalent
after the depopulation caused by the Thirty Years' War and
which formed the subject of the first protective legislation by
the central government in favor of the peasants.

In the period after 1740 the claim of the nobles to the basic
ownership of all lands in their domain, rustic and domestic,
bought and unbought, raised a heated controversy. " Is it not
nonsense to believe," wrote Joseph II, " that the landowners
possessed land before subjects existed, and that they then,
under certain conditions, conferred what was their own upon

6 Ignaz Beidtel, " Zur Geschichte der Feudalverfassung in den Deutschen
Provinzen der Oesterreichischen Monarchie unter der Regierung der Kaiserin
Maria Theresia," *Akademie der Wissenschaften, Sitzungsberichte der Philo-
sophisch-Historischen Klasse*, Vienna, 1853, XI, 476.

the latter?"[7] As late as 1847 a document of one of the estates quoted this sentence and then added: " What Joseph II called nonsense is the truth."[8]

But in the early eighteenth century no Joseph II existed to ridicule the claims of the nobles; and the peasant, for the privilege of using the land, as well as for a protection which by that time had become largely theoretical, made payments to the nobles in money, kind and work. Of these obligations, labor services were the most oppressive, and while they did not constitute as crushing a burden as in the Slavic provinces and in Hungary, they were onerous enough. As far back as the beginning of the sixteenth century there had been in Austria, as there had been throughout Western Europe, a gradual conversion of services into money payments, but the result of the Peasants' War and, according to Dopsch, the general rise of prices accompanying the influx of precious metals from the New World, made the lords anxious to reverse the trend.[9] Thus by 1740 the peasants were still giving services— or *robot*[10]—although it is hard to know their exact extent since they differed from manor to manor and were as a rule fixed by custom only, if at all.[11]

Typically the services consisted not only of labor in the field but also of such varied functions as running errands, driving coaches, hunting or fishing for the lord, working in his vineyard, or even spinning for him, a task which was to

7 Quoted in Adam Wolf and Hans von Zwiedineck-Südenhorst, *Oesterreich unter Maria Theresia, Joseph II und Leopold II*, Berlin, 1884, p. 267.

8 *Ibid.*, p. 267.

9 A. Dopsch, " Die ältere Wirtschafts -und Sozialgeschichte der Bauern in den Alpenländern Oesterreichs," *Instituttet for Sammenlignende Kulturforskning*, Oslo, 1930, pp. 137-38.

10 *Robot*, the Czech word for work, is used to connote feudal labor services throughout the Habsburg monarchy.

11 Technically there were two kinds of *robot*, limited (*gemessene*), and unlimited (*ungemessene*). The latter, for obvious reasons, was the prevailing type.

become important when later the government attempted to encourage the domestic linen industry. For such services, the peasant did not remain completely unrewarded. He had as a rule the right to use the common pasture, was supplied with building materials and could count on the help of the landowner in years of bad harvest.[12] The nature of dues in kind varied with the tradition and customs of different manors. Typical of earlier times had been the presentation of the best head of cattle (*Besthaupt*) which had been abolished by the *Tractatus de Iuribus Incorporabilibus* of Leopold I (1677), though various other taxes, such as the tax on change of property (*laudemium*), the death tax (*mortuarium*), and all the various forms of the tithe, were still in force at the accession of Maria Theresa.

Dues in money and kind did not end the payments of the peasant, for he also paid the country's taxes. Actually, the constitution of the various provinces gave the estates the right to " divide the taxes among themselves in God-pleasing equality," [13] but it was with more consistency than equality that this service to the fatherland was passed on to the peasants. Historically the basis of taxation was, for Styria, Carinthia, and Carniola, the Register of Landed Property (*Gültbuch*) of 1495, and for Austria that of 1513. In 1543 these provinces agreed on a minimum contribution of 69,045 *Gulden* for Lower Austria, 37,508 *Gulden* for Upper Austria, 72,248 *Gulden* for Styria, 34,824 *Gulden* for Carinthia, and 22,000 *Gulden* for Carniola. But wars and rising prices increased these amounts considerably, and it is estimated that by the end of that century Styria paid four times its original contribution.[14] The taxes were collected by each noble in his own domain, most of the time rigorously, since he himself had to make up defi-

12 I. Beidtel, *Geschichte der Oesterreichischen Staatsverwaltung, op. cit.,* p. 5.

13 Joseph Walter, *Joseph II*, Budweis, 1913, p. 85.

14 F. M. Mayer and H. Pirchegger, *op. cit.,* p. 144.

ciencies. But even the noble with his immediate power came up against a truth which he himself was to turn into a weapon against the Imperial government later in the century, namely that laws which are hated cannot, or at least could not at that period, be fully enforced. Therefore, while the existing tax structure was organized to benefit the nobles, evasion and refusal to pay by the peasant were frequent enough to modify these benefits in some degree.[15]

The lord had, however, one more hold over the peasant, his right of patrimonial justice. Almost all landowners administered civil justice and most of the larger ones criminal justice as well. In fact they often had the power of life and death. In this case, however, they had to obtain a special permission, the so-called *Bannleihe,* from the central government which in the course of time also imposed further restrictions.[16] Nevertheless, even the nominal possession of the right, often proudly manifested by the display of gallows near the manor house, was still a source of great prestige to the nobility, and a sure claim to authority.

As the nobles ruled over their domain individually, they ruled over the province collectively in the assembly of the estates. This noble predominance was not necessarily implied in the theory of provincial representation, but it most certainly existed in practice. Even where burghers were allowed to be present, their right to vote tended to be limited. In Lower Austria, for instance, the Estates consisted of fifteen prelates and the Rector of the University of Vienna, 225 princes, counts, and viscounts (*Freiherrn*) and 115 knights, while the one bourgeois vote was divided between the City of Vienna and eighteen other towns and market places. In Styria the story was much the same. The first estate was made up of ten Styrian prelates, the Bishops of Laibach and Lavant who had

15 Karl Biedermann, *Deutschland im 18ten Jahrhundert*, Leipzig, 1880, I, 218.

16 Arnold Luschin von Ebengreuth, *Grundriss der Oesterreichischen Reichsgeschichte*, Bamberg, 1889, p. 275 and p. 278.

possessions in the province, and also deputies from the German Order and the Order of Malta. The nobles were represented by two princes, forty counts and viscounts, and forty knights, while on the other hand sixteen towns and twenty market places shared one vote. As a rule, the estates met only once a year and then their main purpose was to " consent to vote " the direct taxes which the *Hofkommissar,* sent by the central government, demanded of them. But during the year, their standing committee, the so-called *Landesausschuss,* whose point of view was almost without exception that of the nobles, governed the country. There were, of course, even before the reign of Maria Theresa, Imperially appointed officials in the province to advise the committee, but any vigorous centralizing activity seems to have been almost totally lacking.[17] This is perhaps not surprising. Most of the reign of Charles VI, Maria Theresa's predecessor, was concerned with obtaining signatures for the Pragmatic Sanction, ensuring the succession of the House of Habsburg through the female line. The estates of the various Austrian provinces held out long before they signed, demanding concessions. It would have been most imprudent to offend them by centralizing the administration, by curbing the power of the great nobles.

It seems, moreover, that the Pragmatic Sanction was Charles' only real political interest. To stage a successful play at the Favorita,[18] to find just the right kind of wine into which to dip the biscuits for his favorite parrot,[19] appears to have been of greater importance to him than so banal an activity as governing the country well.

17 Ignaz Beidtel, *Geschichte der Oesterreichischen Staatsverwaltung,* *op. cit.,* pp. 13-14.

18 Lady Mary Wortley Montague, *Letters from the Levant,* London, 1838, p. 32.

19 Karl Biedermann, *op. cit.,* I, 228-29.

And while Charles impressed foreign visitors with the magnificence of his household and his " dear, good " [20] wife dazzled them with her beauty, the majority of his subjects lived unspectacular and dreary lives, sometimes on the domain of some overlord but most often in villages.

The creation of the village unit, ascribed by Justi to the " unfortunate law of the fist " [21] of the middle ages, had given rise to, and prolonged, the division of the fields into strips. The prevailing form was the three-field system, although a four or five-field arrangement was not unknown. In the Alpine regions, the fieldgrass system, a very primitive form of cultivation, consisting simply of a more or less regular rotation between tillage and grazing, also existed.[22] Problems and disputes as to the use of peasant land were as a rule settled by the peasants themselves who were expected to turn to the headman of the village, the so-called *Dorfrichter*, for advice.

People who grew grain and raised sheep were, however, not the only people whom eighteenth-century Austrian society regarded as peasants. There were also the wine peasant (*Weinbauer, Winzer,* or *Berghold*) and the wood peasant, the latter being occupied with " loading wood, burning charcoal, cutting trees, and raising cattle, etc." [23] The differentiation of the rural population, however, did not stop here. Among the more respectable members of the rural society we find millers, bakers, butchers, and innkeepers fulfilling important functions in the community. Almost as notable, although much less honorable was the vocation of the skinner (*Abdecker*) who was concerned with disposing of dead horses and

---

20 Oswald Redlich, " Die Tagebücher Karl VI," *Gesamtdeutsche Vergangenheit*, Munich, 1938, p. 144.

21 J. H. G. von Justi, *Oeconomische Schriften*, Berlin, 1760, p. 212.

22 Theodor von der Goltz, *Geschichte der Deutschen Landwirtschaft*, Stuttgart, 1902, p. 247.

23 J. J. Czikam and F. Gräffle (eds.), *Oesterreichische Nationalenzyclopedie*, Vienna, 1835, p. 206.

cattle. Low in the scale also were the agricultural laborers, servants to the more well-to-do peasants. To the former, little attention was paid by anybody in the eighteenth century, except that they amazed everybody who came into contact with them by the rapidity with which they reproduced their species in and out of wedlock.

The problems faced by these peasants were as diverse as were their functions. One very serious difficulty was the wood shortage which made itself definitely felt by the middle of the eighteenth century and which was to become a matter of stringent legislation. Locust plagues and cattle diseases were even more immediately onerous and often catastrophic to the individual. As in all of European society the lack of sanitation and of medical knowledge resulted in the spread of diseases, of which smallpox was probably the most widespread and the most ravaging. To add to the trouble, vagabonds, the " scum " or " pushpeople " (*Schubspersonen*) as they were to be officially called in Austrian legislation, roamed the country, not only making the roads unsafe and travel and mail service extremely hazardous, but also spreading disease. As their name *Schubspersonen* indicated, the time-honored method used by the government and by the local administration was to push these people from one place to the other, a not very effective method of solving the problem that they created.

Drink, then as now, was a way to forget. It was often encouraged by the lords who were likely to possess the franchise for the sale of liquor and as a rule were the direct or indirect owners of inns and taverns. But alcoholic solace had its drawbacks. Peasants with the lord's liquor inside them tended to become boisterous, immoral and often downright dangerous, so that a village baptism, wedding, or even funeral quite often became an occasion to be feared.[24]

---

24 The material for the foregoing five paragraphs was in the main taken from the preambles and descriptions of conditions in subsequent legislation and could therefore not be footnoted in detail.

THE NATURE OF SERFDOM

Thus the position of the Austrian peasantry in 1740 was by no means a happy one. The peasants were hedged in by legal restrictions and, on the whole, they were poor. Perhaps they cannot be regarded as serfs anywhere in the monarchy, especially in the German provinces, although whether they were serfs or not depends on what we accept as a definition of the term. Gruenberg, who says that they were not serfs, defines serfdom as slavery.[25] Joseph II, by virtue of the Decree of Abolition, defined it as the absence of freedom of movement, of freedom of marriage, and of the right to learn a profession according to one's choice.[26] If we accept this latter meaning, *Leibeigenschaft* (serfdom) existed in most of the German Austrian provinces, although it might be questionable whether the fact that the peasants had to pay a fee and get the lord's permission on leaving his domain, can be considered as a complete lack of freedom of movement. Moreover, the disciples of the Knapp-Gruenberg school of thought maintain that the legal status of the peasant, his right to sue and be sued, made him a personally free human being, and therefore not a serf, which is again true if one does not forget how greatly modified this freedom was by the restrictions of patrimonial justice. The controversy is a very old one. Professor Theodor Schmalz, writing in the *Annalen des Königreichs Preussen* (*Annals of the Kingdom of Prussia*) in 1792, claimed for Prussia, as Gruenberg was to claim later for pre-Josephian Austria, that the status of the peasants was one of hereditary subjection (*Erbuntertänigkeit*) and not of serfdom. But the assertion did not go unchallenged even then. " Never did the newer Europe," answered an anonymous writer, " know slavery, except for Negro slaves and Turkish

---

25 Karl Gruenberg, *Bauernbefreiung*, Leipzig, 1894, I, 87.

26 *Handbuch aller unter der Regierung Kaiser Joseph II für die K. K. Erbländer ergangenen Verordnungen und Gesetze*, Vienna, 1785, I, 74 ff. This work is hereafter cited as *Handbuch*.

prisoners-of-war; serfdom never consisted of anything but the obligation to give dues and services on a certain landed estate and not to leave it without the permission of the lord. Where," he continued, " is then the difference between our hereditary subjection and serfdom? Both," he concluded categorically, " mean and are one and the same." [27]

This may seem definite enough. There is, however, one more argument on the Knapp - Gruenberg side, namely that the term serfdom (*Leibeigenschaft*) was so foreign to Austrian legislation that it appeared only three times in Bohemian legislation before Joseph II used it. Yet, the absence of the term does not necessarily preclude the absence of the condition, especially since legislation involving the whole status of the peasant was undoubtedly rare before 1780. And while the term may have been alien to Austrian legislation it was by no means alien to Austrian economic literature. Johann Joachim Becher, the greatest of the seventeenth-century cameralists and, according to Heckscher, " by far the most important " [28] of all German mercantilists, not only recognized the status but accepted and defended it." As far as serfdom is concerned," he wrote in his *Politische Discurs,* " it is of two kinds, heathen and Christian. The heathen kind is nothing but an unmitigated, tyrannical imprisonment, at war with all the laws of nature. Christian serfdom, however, means that the peasant lives in a village, has been brought up there and has his agricultural or other income. In this case I say that, if he is treated in a Christian manner, it is his duty to stay there." [29]

The Peasantry and Cameralism

While Becher was thus defending the subjection of the peasant, he and others like him were sowing the seeds for a

---

27 *Leibeigenschaft,* n. d., p. 542.

28 Eli. F. Heckscher, *Mercantilism,* Mendel Shapiro trans., London, 1935, I, 25.

29 Johann Joachim Becher, *Politische Discurs,* Frankfurt, 1688, pp. 45-6.

development which in its maturity was to become the strongest force for peasant liberation: the rise of a powerful, mercantilist, anti-corporate central government. Perhaps it is true of central governments, as has been said of the bourgeoisie in a similar context, that they are always rising. Attempts by the Habsburg government to dominate the nobles had been made in the middle ages. The victory of Ferdinand II in the counter-reformation is usually viewed as a substantial victory for the central power, but the classic formulation of Austrian centralist philosophy took place in the economic depression following the Thirty Years' War, in the reign of Ferdinand's grandson Leopold.

Probably the most famous work to come out of this period, although it may justifiably be held to have been the least brilliant, was Philipp Wilhelm von Hornick's *Oesterreich über Alles wann es nur will* (*Austria Above Everything if She Only Wishes It*). The title of the book perhaps more than its content accounts for its great popularity and influence. The main thesis of the work itself was that Austria must organize internally in order to achieve the strongest possible position as against foreign countries. In suggesting means to this end, the author catalogued the main principles of Austrian mercantilist thought, a list in which he characteristically gave agriculture the first place and a very brief treatment:

> First it is important to know and observe the nature of the country most exactly, and to consider every single corner and clod of earth, as to whether it can be cultivated or not. Nothing under the sun shall be left untried, if ... it can serve the country, ...

In typically seventeenth-century style he continued: "Before all other things, no pains or trouble are to be avoided to bring gold and silver above the earth." [30] This passage is illuminating

---

30 P. W. von Hornick, *Oesterreich über Alles, wann es nur will*, Regensburg, 1727, p. 29.

in many ways. It shows the mercantilist regard for precious metals. It also indicates the breadth of the seventeenth-century concept of agriculture which included all that had the remotest connection with production from the soil. Most important perhaps it shows how greatly the productive side of agriculture was emphasized, and how little its social side was considered.

None of the other Austrian cameralists, however, was quite as oblivious to the existence of human relationships as Hornick. Wilhelm von Schröder, though he hated the " mob," was at least aware of its existence. His advice to the prince to collect precious metals was predicated upon the fact that, if the prince should ever be in need, nobody would come to his aid : " for the love of the subject is like a limping dog with which one can catch no hare." [31] Yet he advised the prince to treat his people well, for :

> if the father of the family wishes to have a good harvest he must fertilize the acre and plough it; the cattle must be fattened if he wants to slaughter them, and the cows must be fed if he wishes that they shall give much milk. Thus the prince must first help his subjects to a good livelihood if he wants to take something from them.[32]

What to do to fatten the cows was now the problem. And the cosmopolitan, widely-traveled Schröder, Fellow of the Royal Society of London, upon whom the changes brought about by the expansion of Europe overseas had made a deep impression, hit upon an ingenious solution: to introduce Negro and Turkish slaves to lighten the lot of the Austrian peasant :

> I see no reason why we should not make slaves of such barbarians and unbelievers and of the Turkish prisoners-of-war as stubborn enemies of Christianity. They would do the same to us. We ought to drive them to market and sell them in

---

31 Wilhelm von Schroeder, *Fürstliche Schatz- und Rentkammer*, Königsberg, 1752, p. 1.

32 *Ibid.*, preface, xi.

order that everybody who cares to use their services can do so. By that means hard work and agricultural labor could be done by slaves, while the Christians could devote themselves to manufacture.[33]

This proposal seemed to Schröder especially profitable since slaves ate worse food than Christians, could be driven to work and did not have to be paid for their labor. But the matter had its difficulties. The Austrian peasants, as he well realized, were not exactly paragons of tenderness toward their Christian agricultural laborers. What, therefore, would a pagan have to expect? He warned the prospective slaveholders that

> one should not, as is now happening imprudently, let them die of hunger or perish in lice: for though they are Turkish prisoners-of-war they are yet human beings, and if one does not wish to be considerate of them in any other way one should yet accord to them the right of irrational cattle. Neither an ox nor a horse can work long without sufficient amounts of food. It is folly to make these poor imprisoned people perish deliberately, for we deprive ourselves of their services. They should be given enough food and drink in order to remain healthy, strong, and fit to work.[34]

But not all of Schröder's discourse is unusual. At one place or another in his writings all the well-known cameralist precepts such as the cultivation of " wide wastelands and wild heaths,"[35] the planting of tobacco and hemp, and the breeding of cattle and silkworms are suggested to improve the agriculture and therefore the wealth and status of the country.

Yet even here his method of advocacy is as sophisticated as Hornick's was simple. Examples from all lands and all centuries are hauled out from the dark corners of history to prove his point. Constantine the Great is called to witness and so is Charles II's " Act for the Improvement of Tillage and

33 *Ibid.*, p. 206.
34 *Ibid.*, pp. 206-7.
35 *Ibid.*, p. 196.

the Breed of Cattle," [36] until it finally is all summed up in an " advice to the prince " which reads:

> Because the fertility of the country is of such importance, the prince shall take the *curam rei rusticae* under his special care and see to it that the land is so well cultivated that the inhabitants not only get their food and drink from it but still have something left over to sell; *hinc omnes qui prudenter Rempublicam instituerunt et gubernarunt agriculturae primas dederunt*. It is for this reason that all those who governed in wisdom have been the patrons of agriculture.[37]

The last of the seventeenth-century cameralists in our discussion, although the first both chronologically and probably intellectually, is that " *Prachtkerl*," as Sombart calls him, " out of whose ingenious spirit creative thoughts sprayed and burst like fireworks " [38]—Johann Joachim Becher. In reading his works, in considering the events of his miserable personal life, one cannot help feeling that Becher lived in the wrong age, or at least in the wrong place at the wrong time. Among the more radical elements of the Reformation period or among the humanitarians of the eighteenth century he might have been happier. He might have been happier even in the seventeenth-century England where he went to die. But the noble Catholic court of Leopold I could never accept the bourgeois convert, and of all his practical work in Austria only one thing seems to have achieved permanence: the introduction of the potato into the diet of the Austrian peasant.

Becher's early work still echoed the sounds of the Reformation period, reinforced perhaps, although we have no proof of it, by what he may have learned on his travels to Holland of the aims of his contemporaries, the Levellers and Diggers, beyond the Channel. In the *Moral Discurs* he speaks of a com-

36 *Ibid.*, p. 197.

37 *Ibid.*, p. 195.

38 Werner Sombart, *Der Moderne Kapitalismus*, Munich, 1921, I, 473.

munity of the truly pious in which one Christian is equal to another, an equality which does not allow one to serve the other, therefore all must be free. In such a state the peasants form the only natural estate. Furthermore, to avoid all inequalities " poverty and riches, property and luxury, money and private capital are abolished. A livelihood is provided as a reward for agricultural work only." [39] How ironic it is to reflect that the man who urged these principles was one of the great advocates of industry and commerce, an inveterate inventor, one of the spiritual fathers of modern capitalism.

In Becher's later writings the mercantilist and the humanitarian blend. His truly Christian community, as he himself realized, was an impossibility in a society cursed by the fall of man. The latter had established a society of classes (*Ständestaat*) and one had to put up with it as best one could. Yet his concept, even of that society was unusual:

> One must realize that there are two kinds of people in a community, the majority who form the community proper and a minority who are their servants. Among the latter we count those in authority ... who, by keeping the people in good order and within the laws of society, enable one man to live beside another. The community does not exist for the benefit of those in authority, but those in authority for the benefit of the community. Other servants of the community are the priests who take care of the soul, as the scholars do of the mind, the doctors, chemists, and barbers, of health, and the soldiers of the body and of the whole town.[40]

Becher's quantitative concept of the importance of different classes in society logically led him to regard the peasants as basic to its whole structure:

39 Emil Kauder, " Johann Joachim Becher," *Schmollers Jahrbuch für Gesetzgebung, Verwaltung und Volkswirtschaft im Deutschen Reich,* Munich, 1924, p. 70.

40 J. J. Becher, *op. cit.,* pp. 4-5.

The peasantry is the greatest estate, for the majority of people must be peasants. Without the labor of the peasant the artisan would have nothing to manufacture, and without those two the merchant would have nothing to trade. Consequently the peasant is not only the foundation of the nobility but of the civil estate and its society.[41]

Becher was apparently never quite certain what the relationship between the peasant and the noble should be. At one point in the *Politische Discurs* he made, as we have seen, a somewhat feeble attempt to defend serfdom. In *Psychosophia,* however, he deplored the discrepancy between natural and formal nobility and the " wicked custom " that " the nobility of today stems more often from a sheet of paper than from its own merit." [42] In a ferociously sarcastic passage he described the " nobleman of current fashion " :

> The more and better he can curse, the less he believes, the better a gentleman, for belief is monkish.
> The more insolent, the more impudent, the angrier, the more tyrannical and presumptuous he is, the better a gentleman.
> The less he studies, the more he knows nothing but how to swear and lie, the better a gentleman.
> The more he drinks, eats, gambles, whores, and tyrannizes, the better a gentleman.
> The more he can haggle, oppress his subjects, shear and flay, and by war, rape, murder, and laying waste take what belongs to others, the more a gentleman.[43]

For the poor subjects of such a lord, Becher had only one advice—to escape to Turkey. And then, under the guise of describing Turkey, a land still sufficiently far away and unknown to lend itself to such a purpose, Becher set up a Utopia in which one would be safe from the molestations of such gentlemen :

41 *Ibid.,* p. 6.

42 J. J. Becher, *Psychosophia*, Hamburg, 1725, p. 57.

43 *Ibid.,* pp. 57-8.

They have no standing there, no power, and cannot exercise the slightest compulsion over the lowest peasant, for the Grand Turk alone is master, and knows of no *subdivisionibus*. Everybody lives in the greatest peace and freedom, in religion and justice. One knows of no internal wars, nor of contributions and excises. Furthermore there is in that country the finest land in the world and enough room for cultivation. The Turks themselves are now quiet, modest, merciful people, the enemies of all cruelty, insolence, and frivolity.[44]

This visionary picture of Turkey, it would seem, represents the cameralist ideal at its best. It is also a clear projection of the kind of Austria Joseph II attempted to build a century later: A benevolent, unified, omnicompetent state, the enemy of all insolence, cruelty and sloth, a foe of the nobility, a partisan of justice, and for all these reasons a firm advocate of the protection and emancipation of the peasant.

44 *Ibid.,* pp. 58 9.

CHAPTER II
THE AGRARIAN REFORMS OF MARIA THERESA

DURING their own lifetime the seventeenth-century cameralists were forced to realize that their preaching had little effect. Had they been able to watch Austria half a century later, they would have found equally little satisfaction. Then a momentous event occurred, one which, as German nationalists, they would probably have decried heartily: the King of Prussia invaded Silesia. The state of Austria at the beginning of the invasion has been often described. Historians on different sides, with different biases, have agreed on the facts of the situation: the ruler of the country was a young woman who, unschooled in the art of politics, had just ascended the throne. The treasury was almost empty; the credit of the country, at a low ebb. Not even the loyalty of the population towards the House of Habsburg could be taken for granted. The stricter measures of government control which the cameralists had advocated now became a practical necessity. A new tax system, bringing in its train a new method of public administration, was the short-run expedient by which the government's financial problem was to be met. Beyond this, there was a gradual realization on the part of Maria Theresa and her advisers that, to prevent the recurrence of a catastrophe like 1740, it was necessary to raise the general level of the health and welfare of the population. This meant the improvement both of agricultural methods and of living conditions in rural areas.

This realization was strengthened by influences from another source. The German philosophy of Natural Rights, stemming from Puffendorf and Christian Wolf, had also made inroads into Austria. It affected, if not Maria Theresa herself, at least some of her advisers, giving to cameralism a new *raison d'être* by gradually changing the focus of its emphasis from the welfare of the prince to the welfare of the people.

POLITICAL THOUGHT AT THE TIME OF MARIA THERESA

The theorist who perhaps represented most perfectly the fusion of these two tendencies was Johann Heinrich Gottlieb von Justi. A prolific writer, a lecturer at the Theresianum at Vienna, he was probably the most influential of Austrian political and economic thinkers of the period. Of the role of the people he spoke in terms similar to Rousseau:

> If a people unite their powers and their will, and leave the use of the united powers to the united will, that is, if they establish a highest power, then this power rests in the beginning indisputably with the people, for it has been created by a union of their powers and their wills. A people can either exercise this power itself, make provisions for its use, or delegate it to others. The power by which a people makes provision for the exercise or delegation of sovereignty is called the *basic power of the people* and differs from active authority which is created only by the provisions of the former. The basic power of the people is an integral part of the nature of the state, and always exists, even when there is the most absolute authority.[1]

Justi was alone, however, in proposing constitutional limitations on the absolute monarchy. Most of the other figures of the "Austrian Enlightenment," the elder van Swieten, Gebler, Sonnenfels, accepted this institution almost as a matter of course. A typical statement of their case is the justification of absolutism put forth in 1768 by Karl Anton von Martini, one-time tutor of the young Archdukes Joseph and Leopold.

Martini, like Justi, accepted a social contract theory, but maintained that once the contract had been concluded the "monarch [was] not merely a caretaker but a ruler in his own right." The subjects, consequently, had no right to re-

---

1 Johann Heinrich Gottlieb von Justi, *Grundriss einer Guten Regierung*, Frankfurt, 1759, pp. 6-7.

sist by force, but only by petition or, if conditions became too unbearable, by flight. Passive resistance by them was allowed only if the monarch showed signs of wishing to ruin the state. In that case, however, he ought to be regarded as insane, and in Martini's eyes " deserved pity rather than hatred." By this masterpiece of logic Martini modified what he called the " bold and groundless " ideas of that " second Diogenes," Rousseau, in order to provide a rationalization for the absolute monarchy of the German princes.[2]

Martini's tortuous logic was possibly made necessary by the realities of the situation. The alternative to absolute monarchy would have been domination by the nobles. Long experience had proved that from the latter the common people could expect little. Any protection, any liberation that would ever come to them was likely to emanate from the central government at Vienna.[3] It would, of course, be a mistake to see in the central monarchy, at least in the time of Maria Theresa, a conscious ally of the common people. Maria Theresa herself was completely part of the nobility in her beliefs and attitudes, and had little thought of overturning a system of which she was so integral a part. But the humanitarian spirit of the eighteenth century was in the air and even the court at Vienna did not altogether escape it. Maria Theresa personally was not greatly affected by it. She substituted a feeling of motherliness towards her subjects and a sense of religious obligation: " For the sake of a few great magnates and nobles," she wrote at the time of the *Urbarial*[4] *Decree for Hungary*, " I shall not risk eternal damnation." [5]

2 Adolf Menzel, " Ein Oesterreichischer Staatsphilosoph des 18ten Jahrhunderts," *Oesterreichische Rundschau*, Vienna, 1905, I, 299.

3 For a more ample treatment of this idea see Fritz Kern, " Vom Herrenstaat zum Wohlfahrtsstaat," *Schmollers Jahrbuch fuer Gesetzgebung, Verwaltung und Volkswirtschaft im Deutschen Reich*, Munich, 1928.

4 *Urbarium*, usually assumed to be a latinization of the German word *urbar* (arable), is used to denote legislation concerning labor services throughout the Habsburg Empire.

5 Henry Marczali, *Hungary in the Eighteenth Century*, Cambridge, 1910, p. 192.

CHARLES VII AND THE ABOLITION OF SERFDOM IN BOHEMIA

When Maria Theresa first turned her attention to the fate of those who tilled the soil, it was for less transcendental reasons. Charles VII, Elector of Bavaria, who had been chosen Emperor by the Electors of the Holy Roman Empire and with Prussian and French support claimed succession to the Habsburg lands, invaded Bohemia in 1742. He called on all the inhabitants of the kingdom to come to his aid. To the peasants he promised that their assistance would be rewarded by the abolition of serfdom and the remittance of taxes for three years. If we can believe Arneth, the major Austrian historian on this period, the court of Vienna was aghast at the impudence of this action.[6] They themselves had been vaguely considering a similar step, but had eventually refrained, concluding that:

> To abolish subjection completely can never be held useful. For there is no country where distinctions between lords and subjects do not exist. To free the latter from duties towards the former would only make one riotous and the other discontented and would, on all sides, trample upon justice.[7]

That another ruler thus dared to "trample upon justice" was incomprehensible to Maria Theresa. In a burst of anger she ordered that the decree be publicly burnt by the hangman. But finally, imbued as she was with the idea of the dignity and inviolability of the princely estate, she thought better of her order. "So far as the executioner is concerned," she added to the rescript, "I am doubtful. Crowned heads always respect one another. The appeal may be burnt, but not by such unworthy hands." [8]

THE NEW TAX SYSTEM

Philosophy and political rivalry may have created a frame of mind favorable to agrarian reform. But the first practical

6 Alfred von Arneth, *Geschichte Maria Theresias*, Vienna, 1864, II, 111.

7 *Ibid.*, II, 489.

8 *Ibid.*, II, 111.

steps were taken for more prosaic reasons, the financial needs of the Austrian state. The war with Prussia was a great drain on a treasury which was already half empty as a result of the wars in the first half of the eighteenth century and the lavish style of living at the court of Charles VI. In 1740 the total debt of the Austrian state was estimated at fifty million *Gulden.*[9] In 1747 Haugwitz, Maria Theresa's chief financial adviser, set it at about 106 million *Gulden.*[10] To Haugwitz a partial solution could be found by an increase in direct taxes. To make certain that this tax should not depend completely upon the good will of the estates, he suggested that the government conclude agreements whereby yearly quotas should be voted for ten years at a time (*Decennalrecess*). To make the increase more palatable to the estates, the central government itself should take over recruiting, quartering and feeding of soldiers, an idea which had military as well as financial advantages. By these expedients the government would be able to obtain about fourteen million *Gulden* instead of the eight to nine million which had been collected each year since 1739.[11] After much calculation in government offices, the desired sum was set at 13,314,826 *Gulden* five *Kreutzer,* of which the German-speaking provinces were to pay about six million *Gulden.*[12]

During the creation of the plan, and in its execution as well, Maria Theresa put complete confidence in Haugwitz. A native of the now conquered part of Silesia he had, in Maria Theresa's words: " Out of loyalty and faith left everything in Silesia and stood by me in evil times." [13] Uprooted, thrown

9 Franz von Mensi, *Die Finanzen Oesterreichs,* Vienna, 1890, p. 700.

10 Adolf Beer, " Staatsschulden und die Ordnung des Staatshaushaltes unter Maria Theresia," *Archiv fuer Oesterreichische Geschichte,* Vienna, 1895, LXXXII, 88.

11 F. von Mensi, *op. cit., table,* p. 474.

12 A. Beer, *op. cit.,* pp. 99-100.

13 A. von Arneth (ed.), "Zwei Denkschriften der Kaiserin Maria Theresia," *Archiv fuer Oesterreichische Geschichte,* Vienna, 1871, XLVII, 269 ff.

completely upon the mercy of the court at Vienna for his success in life, he was an ideal civil servant. " He was," wrote Maria Theresa, " truly sent to me by Providence." [14]

After having arranged for a *Decennalrecess* in Bohemia and and Moravia, Haugwitz was sent as a government deputy to the Estates of Lower Austria which met on July 14, 1748. There was much wrangling, but eventually the estates agreed to almost all the demands of the government. In confirming the agreement by the law of September 18, 1748, the Empress expressed the belief that the program would benefit not only the government but the peasantry as well:

> We have taken into our most gracious consideration that the quartering, military contribution, services, . . . as well as the sometimes oppressive board and extras have become a great burden. No less do we realize how hard it is to provide recruits, horses, and the necessary requisitions. It is easy to recognize, therefore, that if all these duties remained as they were under the old constitution, the subject, oppressed in so many ways, would be ruined, and the tax system necessarily disrupted.[15]

As an example of the kind of reasoning which led to peasant emancipation in Austria, this passage is typical. It makes a great show of humanitarian feeling and of fighting the oppression of the peasantry, and then goes on to say that all this is necessary to facilitate the collection of taxes. We meet similar statements again and again in Austrian reform legislation before Joseph II. There is a kind of brutality in this blunt admission, or perhaps just a refreshing frankness. At any rate the government never for a moment attempted to deceive anybody about the final aim of its actions. Yet in many branches of the administration at Vienna, there was genuine

14 *Ibid.*, p. 308.

15 I. Beidtel, *op. cit.*, p. 26.

concern for the fate of the peasantry. To us this may seem to be a contradiction. The men of the eighteenth century probably did not consider it as such. They believed in a pre-established harmony between the good and the useful, and saw no reason why the material advantage of the state could not be synchronized with the welfare of the population. During the reign of Maria Theresa these two motives went side by side, were intertwined, and only in the time of Joseph II did the second prevail.

The good of the state and the welfare of the population demanded that the peasants should no longer be the sole taxpayers. Here also the decree of September 18, 1748, expressed a new philosophy: " To facilitate the collection of this sum [the quota for Lower Austria amounting to 2,008,908 *Gulden* 44 *Kreutzer* and 2½ *Pfennig*] a just equality in its division would be most useful." [16]

Theoretically, and again this is typical of Maria Theresa's whole approach to the problem of centralization, the right of the nobles to levy and collect taxes continued to be recognized. For in this same patent the Empress promised " not to publish any decree concerning the contribution without the consent of the estates " and to declare the taxes she was to receive as an obligation " freely consented to." [17]

The *Decennalrecess* with the Estates of Lower Austria was the most successful attempt by the government to centralize the tax administration in the German provinces. In the Inner Austrian lands (Styria, Carinthia and Carniola) which were, as Maria Theresa said in one of her memoranda, always in financial difficulties, the government met with determined opposition. These provinces steadfastly refused to approve a ten-year advance. Styria finally accepted a three-year recess, and Carniola followed suit a year later. In Carinthia, however,

16 *Ibid.*, p. 27.
17 *Ibid.*, p. 28.

" nothing was to be done." [18] The Estates did not want to hear of any " God-pleasing equality " and insisted that the increased tax burden should be placed entirely upon the peasants. Finally Maria Theresa saw herself forced to resort to a device which she disliked greatly, but which her son was to use extensively during his own reign, namely legislation by royal fiat.

> Since the estates could not be brought to accept any reasonable ideas, I saw myself forced to collect the sum *jure Regio* ... During the previous year they had given Count Rudolf Choteck a signed recess, but had repealed it a year later, their constant lament being that they could not afford the amount. They would not, however, save anything in their domestic and other administrative funds, but proposed, either in ignorance or in malice, that the subjects should be burdened still further. This is why I ordered the collection of the sum *jure Regio*.[19]

In Tyrol, the traditional backbone of particularist opposition to the central government, the recess could be concluded for a year only. This fact has led Guglia, one of the main authorities on the period of Maria Theresa, to believe that the significance of the new tax system was not primarily in the agreements on the recesses. He finds its main importance in the fact that the exemption of the nobles from taxation had, in theory at least, been eliminated, that the recruiting, quartering, and provisioning of soldiers became the task of the state, and that, in general, the role of the state in tax collection had been greatly extended.[20]

In the *Sistemalpatent* of 1748, which recapitulated the whole question for the purpose of positive legislation, the peasant protective aspects of the system were again emphasized:

18 A. v. Arneth, " Zwei Denkschriften der Kaiserin Maria Theresia," *op. cit.*, p. 315.

19 *Ibid.*, p. 315.

20 E. Guglia, *op. cit.*, II, 9.

The contribution directly assigned to the estates may not be mingled with taxes to be paid by the subjects. Neither should the subjects be burdened with taxes due from those rustic lands which are in the hands of the lord ... In assessing the sum to be paid by the ordinary tax-payer, special care ought to be taken that he be made to contribute a greater sum in good, and a smaller in bad months. In the second case the landowner ought to be made to contribute more. In this fashion an equality of payment can be established in every month.[21]

At the same time the government, quite well aware of the customary inefficiency of tax collection in Austria, decided to turn over a new leaf in that direction also. The twenty-first of every month was to be the last day for all monthly payments. Those peasants who had not met the deadline were "to be covered with military execution." This forbidding phrase did not quite mean that the peasant would be beheaded if he defaulted. It is rather a phrase used in eighteenth century Austria to denote the legal seizure of goods as a method of enforcing payment. The confiscations were carried out by the militia. If a peasant's refusal to meet his obligations was thought to be deliberate, the number of soldiers sent to perform the task was doubled. This policy seems to have resulted in regular *dragonnades* and apparently was greatly feared by the peasantry.

The *Sistemalpatent* also showed a new strictness with the nobles: "As far as the nobles are concerned, real sequestration without distinction of persons shall take place, incomes shall be blocked, existing stores sold, and government administrators be appointed as sequestrators of the manorial income."

In order to have a law executed in eighteenth-century Austria, it was not enough to threaten with punishment those who disobeyed it. One had to threaten the executors as well. True to form the *Sistemalpatent* provided that all officials in-

21 Sammlung, *op. cit.*, I, 71-91.

volved in tax collection, village headmen, manorial officials and accountants, should be " covered with military execution " and even arrested if they failed in their duty.

In its closing paragraph the law again affirmed the primary role of the peasant in the whole scheme: " Finally the greatest number . . . of ordinary taxpayers consists of the village subjects or peasants who, before all others, are to be protected by their lord from the oppression of the officials and the evil conduct of the tax collectors."

While the government laid down the principles by which the sum it demanded ought to be divided among the various estates, it did not interfere with the subdivision of this sum among individual tax payers. Nor did it take over tax collection. This was a substantial victory for the nobles who, being, in this respect at least, the actual executors of the law, found it in many instances easy to circumvent the measure.

Maria Theresa and her advisers probably realized how much they had weakened the effectiveness of their law by not taking over the actual assessment and collection of taxes, but there was little they could have done. When Joseph II later attempted to do away with both privileges, he almost faced a noble revolt.

Maria Theresa did, however, try to provide a more just and equal basis for the assessment of taxes. For this purpose she had a new land survey (*cadastre*) drawn up. The main aim of this survey was to make the distinction between peasant land and noble land so clear that the lord could not claim peasant land under any pretext. In this instance the social and the fiscal motive met. The state was undoubtedly interested in preserving peasant land for the peasantry. But it was probably even more concerned with the higher tax rates paid on land registered as peasant property.

It was clear from the beginning that the new law would not have smooth sailing. Already in the summer of 1749 it was decreed that communities which did not pay their taxes were to be immediately investigated.[22] In the inquiries which followed it was apparently discovered that, not only non-payment of taxes by the subject, but at times non-delivery by collecting officials caused the slowness of tax returns. The law for Upper and Lower Austria of August 2, 1753 found it necessary to threaten that if

> in the future the headman of a village dares to embezzle tax money, the manorial lord shall immediately denounce him to the local administration and have him sent to jail at his own expense. His property shall be estimated and sold. The proceeds shall be used to satisfy the claims of the tax office. If this is omitted the negligent lord shall be obliged to indemnify the treasury.[23]

The collecting officials were not the only authorities whose honesty was called into question. A law of April 14, 1770 deplored the fact that the lords often asked interest from their subjects on taxes that were paid after the twenty-first of the month and demanded that " this nonsense be discontinued on pain of the most severe punishment." [24]

A law of the following year called on manorial and Imperial administrative officials not to permit peasants to waste wheat and other farm products and on that basis pay a smaller amount of taxes. The same law, however, absolutely forbade that peasants be forced to sell cattle to meet tax obligations.[25] This benevolence may have been only a selfish speculation for future gain. But then perhaps " enlightened self-interest " has been the basis for the greatest and most durable reforms.

The stern determination by the central government paid dividends. Despite vocal opposition and silent sabotage from many quarters, the financial reforms of Maria Theresa were

22 *Ibid.*, I, 116.
23 *Ibid.*, I, 175.
24 *Ibid.*, VI, 189.
25 *Ibid.*, VI, 424-25.

successful. In 1754 the Prussian Ambassador Fuerst estimated that the income which Austria derived from direct taxes amounted to about sixteen million *Gulden*.[26] In 1773 Schloezer, one of the most respected publicists of the time, set it at 19,-700,000 *Gulden*.[27] Towards the end of Maria Theresa's reign Councillor Greiner, father of Karoline Pichler and one of the government's financial experts, unequivocally testified to the success of the reform when he wrote to Maria Theresa:

> What found more opposition than the Haugwitz tax system? Were not all ministers, even the most experienced and intelligent, willing to stake their lives on a bet that the country would not be able to carry this exorbitant burden for six years. Now almost thirty years have passed and the country carries not only the Haugwitz contribution but nearly twice as much.[28]

ADMINISTRATIVE AND JUDICIAL REFORMS

Administration. The tax reforms of Maria Theresa could hardly have been a success had it not been for another series of reforms which again affected drastically the existing landowner-peasant relationship.

During the reign of Maria Theresa reforms in civil and political administration took place on all levels. On the top level there was the unification of the Austrian and Bohemian Chancellery into the *directorium in publicis et cameralibus,* the founding of the High Court of Justice, and in 1760 the formation of the Council of State. The formation of these bodies affected the peasantry only in as far as they served as policy-making organs.

The rural population was most directly affected, however, by the administrative re-organization on the provincial level.

26 Leopold von Ranke, "Maria Theresia," *Historisch-Politische Zeitschrift*, Berlin, 1833-36, II, 708.

27 August L. Schloezer, *Briefwechsel*, Goettingen, 1780, II, 244.

28 Alfred von Arneth, "Maria Theresia und der Hofrath von Greiner," *Kaiserliche Akademie der Wissenschaften, Sitzungsberichte der Philosophisch-Historischen Klasse*, Vienna, 1859, XXX, 329.

Kreisaemter (subdivisions of the provincial government or *Gubernium*) had existed in Bohemia as local bodies for a long time. They were now introduced into the German provinces (and re-organized in the Slavic countries) as agencies of the central government. Apparently the first mention of the new institution was in the patent on taxation addressed to the Estates of Styria, Carinthia, and Carniola on October 6, 1748. In it we hear that it is the function of its officials to take care of the quartering and provisioning of troops and also to see that the lords do not overburden the subjects but keep them " in a taxable state." If a justified complaint arose the subjects were to " turn to the . . . *Kreisamt* officials employed in every district of the country." The latter were instructed that it was not enough " that these subjects obtained the satisfaction due to them. The guilty lord or his steward [was] to be fined severely." [29]

In Lower Austria these local governments were introduced five years later, on July 24, 1753, and in Tyrol, in June 1754. Perhaps as a concession to the conservatism of that mountain population, they there retained the name of the former local organs controlled by the Estates, *Viertelkommissare* (district commissioners).[30]

The patent to the Estates of Inner Austria had clearly stated what the government set out to do in reorganizing the administration: to protect the peasants and keep them in taxable condition. If the new system was to work it was necessary to take away the administrative functions of the lord and his officials and to assign them to the new institution. This was done by a gradual and, on the whole, unspectacular process. From the beginning the *Kreisaemter* were to supervise the tax system. Over the years they also received authority to deal with vagabond problems, donations, rural hospitals, domestic servants, forest affairs, and a host of minor problems which

29 E. Guglia, *op. cit.*, II, 34.

30 *Ibid.*, II, 35.

hitherto had not been taken care of by any particular agency. If, for instance, a peasant invented something beneficial to the progress of agriculture and industry, and could not win recognition or compensation for it from his lord, he was to bring the matter to the attention of the *Kreisamt*.[31]

Repeatedly the government sent out circulars to enumerate the functions of these local governments. Sometimes these writs were of very general, at other times of more specific character. In general it was explained that it was the duty of the district officials to fulfill "her Majesty's orders reliably, to keep good order, and to look after everything concerning the public welfare." [32]

Other instructions were more precise. The decree of July 4, 1770 specifically laid down the rules which the local governments were to follow in protecting the peasant against the lord. They were to supervise the Book of Contributions, to make certain that the peasant was free to sell his produce in the free market, and to ensure that he would not be forced to give the lord a right of pre-emption on his agricultural products. Finally they were to restrain the lord from inflicting very severe corporal punishments or fines on the peasants.[33]

Few laws are meaningful, few reforms successful, unless a competent bureaucracy sees to their application. The record of the House of Habsburg in training an officialdom of that kind had been rather poor up to the accession of Maria Theresa. During her reign a valiant effort was made to remedy the situation. After 1776 nobody was to be accepted for service with the local government unless he was experienced in administrative and " cameral " sciences.[34] To improve the officials' relations to the peasantry, the former were asked to express

31 *Sammlung, op. cit.,* V, 162.

32 Theodor von Kern, " Die Reformen der Kaiserin Maria Theresia," *Historisches Taschenbuch,* Leipzig, 1869, p. 117.

33 *Sammlung, op. cit.,* VI, 255.

34 *Ibid.,* V, 59.

themselves simply and without the use of Latin since otherwise the " headmen and elders of the village would not understand them." [35] Stiff penalties were announced for all officials
who accepted presents from members of the community,[36] and
all " understandings and partialities " between Imperial and
manorial officials were prohibited.[37] Eventually a decree of
April 17, 1776 forbade employees of the local government
from accepting food from the lord's steward without payment.[38]

The repeated laws attempting to prohibit collusion between
the lord and his officials on the one hand and Imperial func-
tionaries on the other, show that such practices must have
been frequent. This was only natural. The lower officials in
the government as a rule belonged to the upper bourgeoisie
or lower nobility themselves and tended to have more in
common with the lord's officials and the local gentry than with
anybody else in the district. The situation concerning the
Kreisamt heads was even more unfortunate. Almost without
exception they were members of the old provincial nobility. In
1753 we find as the heads of local governments in Lower Austria a Count Herberstein, a *Freiherr* von Pilati, a von Hager,
a von Sondersleben;[39] in Tyrol, a Baron Ceschi a Santa Croce,
a von Franzin and a Baron Vogelmeier.[40] The effectiveness
of the legislation of Maria Theresa depended on whether or
not such men as these would put the Imperial interest before
that of their own class. Their position was not always an easy
one. If they fulfilled the intentions of the Imperial house too
well, their fellow aristocrats were apt to denounce them as
traitors to the " well-earned liberties " of the nobility. If on

35 *Ibid.*, III, 353.

36 *Ibid.*, V, 404-5.

37 *Ibid.*, VI, 407.

38 *Ibid.*, VII, 516-18.

39 E. Guglia, *op. cit.*, II, 36.

40 Joseph Eger, *Geschichte Tirols*, Innsbruck, 1889, III, 36.

the other hand, they were mindful of these " well-earned liberties," they tended to incur the displeasure of the court at Vienna. In the provinces the opponents of the central government tended to outweigh its friends. In the government offices at Vienna the distribution was about equal. It must be remembered that such categorization is relative. Under Maria Theresa the alternatives were not yet clearly formulated. Few accepted the fact that such a choice had to be made. Within certain limits, which were often fairly broad, many members of the nobility were willing to support the aims of the central administration. The support which such men were willing to give to the program of the Imperial government accounts for much of its success. Maria Theresa clearly realized this when, in what one enthusiastic historian called " her beautiful judgment about the profession of provincial officials," [41] she wrote: " It is always the fault of those provincial officials who do not do their duty . . . Thus countries go to ruin." [42]

Justice. In the history of the Austrian state, justice and administration had long formed one branch of government. After 1740 prevailing political thought, as well as the reforms which began to take place in the field of political and civil administration, prompted Maria Theresa to attempt a separation. Justice, she thought, would improve greatly under the new scheme. In a well-known memorandum she spoke of this separation as the " true corner-stone through which I may sustain the monarchy entrusted to me by God, for Whose further sturdy assistance we all hope, for the benefit and best interest of my posterity." Such a separation would give the sovereign an opportunity to examine the grievances of his subjects, to " further a just and God-pleasing procedure between lords and subjects, and to watch carefully that the poor, and especi-

41 Th. Kern, *op. cit.*, p. 199.

42 A. v. Arneth, " Maria Theresia und der Hofrath von Greiner," *op. cit.*, p. 339.

ally the subjects, are not oppressed by the rich, and especially by the lords." [43]

The most important measure in the field of justice against such oppression was the law of December 22, 1769 which provided that, " although the lords have the right to maintain courts of the first instance and to handle cases involving their subjects, that is, have the right to civil justice, the punishment shall not be imposed, and consequently the subject not be jailed, until the provincial government is informed about the case and has approved the patrimonial decision." [44]

While by this decree the government definitely limited the lord's right to patrimonial justice, it defined, by the Patent of February 29, 1772, the manner in which the peasant could bring complaints against his master. It was however, careful to point out that this did not mean a blanket endorsement of of the subjects' claims against the lord, and threatened those peasants who showed " stubbornness, obstinacy, disorder, wickedness, wantonness, or would even dare to take part in mob gatherings and uprisings " with the most severe punishment.[45]

THE REFORM OF LABOR SERVICES

The wish to avoid such unrest among the rural population, coupled with the realization that, if the financial needs of the state were to be met, a reduction of the peasant's dues and services to the lord had to take place, led to legislation on labor services in Austria. We find the origins of this policy not in the German provinces, but in Hungary, where cruel and ruthless suppression of the peasants seems to have been the order of the day. After the first regulations there, which achieved little more than the most elementary degree of peasant protection, the center of attention shifted to the little

43 A. v. Arneth, " Zwei Denkschriften der Kaiserin Maria Theresia," *op. cit.*, p. 323.

44 *Sammlung, op. cit.*, V, 479.

45 *Ibid.*, VIII, 534-40.

Austrian remnant of Silesia, where peasant revolts had broken out in the neighborhood of Bielitz and Teschen. It was over the Silesian question that we find the first outspoken formulation of policy by Maria Theresa and her advisers. From the beginning these advisers were split on fundamental questions. While the majority, among them the head of the commission, Locella, stood for the traditional rights and privileges of the nobility, Franz Anton von Blank attacked historical traditions in the name of natural law. To him the most important factor was not what existed, but what ought to exist. The plan he postulated called for a limitation, as well as a regulation, of dues and services.[46] Despite her regard for established institutions, the Empress agreed with him and much of what he had suggested was incorporated into the Silesian *robot* patent of 1771.

The Reform of Labor Services in Lower Austria. The next year saw the publication of a similar regulation for Lower Austria. As the initial trial ground for the reform in the German provinces, Lower Austria was a good choice. There, if anywhere, it would be a success. The peasantry in Lower Austria was less oppressed than that of most other provinces. The Estates, which had their seat at Vienna, were loyal to the Imperial house, docile, probably the least rebellious nobility in the monarchy. The government's expectations were to prove justified. Except for minor objections, the law was accepted without difficulty.

The law itself was long and detailed. It began by defining those who were obliged to perform labor services: " Each vassal or subject in the country, of whatever station he may be, is obliged to do week work for the landlord for each inhabited holding." [47] For land without houses no services were

46 Karl Grünberg, " Franz Anton von Blank," *Schmollers Jahrbuch für Gesetzgebung, Verwaltung und Volkswirtschaft im Deutschen Reich,* Leipzig, 1911, p. 133.

47 Ferdinand von Hauer, *Praktische Darstellung der in Oesterreich unter der Enns für das Unterthansfach Bestehenden Gesetze,* Vienna, 1824, I, 82.

demanded. The services were to be discharged either by the owner of the farm himself, or by any fit person, " consequently by one neither so young nor so old, or otherwise so weak, as to be unable to perform the task assigned." If there were several persons on a holding, only one could be called to perform the services.[48]

Regarding the performance of week work the decree provided that:

> Since in this part of the country the subjects have, so far as week work is concerned, traditionally been divided into whole, half, and quarter tenants, such a division is to be maintained. A whole tenant has the duty to drive to the fields with a four animal team, a half tenant with a two animal team. The teams can consist of either horses or oxen. The fact that a tenant might own a greater number of teams should in no way increase his burden. On the other hand, all whole or half tenants are obliged to perform their services with teams, even if they do not own any. A quarter tenant is to perform personal services only.[49]

The provision that the peasants were to perform their services with teams, even if they did not own any, must have been somewhat baffling to those who were asked to perform that feat. The issue was decided by a resolution of November 6, 1773, which decreed that all whole and half tenants were obliged to keep horses and oxen for labor duty even if they did not need them for their own farm. On the other hand, the patent of 1772 had granted the lords the right to ask for services by hand instead of with teams if they so desired.[50]

The oldest grievance of the peasantry with regard to week work had been its unregulated nature and the fact that the peasant usually spent more time on the lord's domain than on his own. In Lower Austria both conditions had been rare

48 *Ibid.*, I, 84.
49 *Ibid.*, I, 95-6.
50 *Ibid.*, I, 88.

even before the new law. The decree of 1772 aimed to make them impossible. The number of days during which week work could be demanded was limited to 104 per year for all categories of peasants except *Inleute* (peasants who lived on the manor and owned no property). Although the latter could not be made to pay any other fees, they were to perform labor services for twelve days a year. They were to discharge this duty even if they worked as artisans.

After the law of 1772 had limited the number of working days to 104 a year, it went on to confine them to two a week, except in those cases where previous days had been missed. The "sacred Sundays and commanded holidays" were exempted completely. Finally, the working day was limited to twelve hours, ten for actual labor and two for feeding men and animals.

Thus the patent set a maximum on labor services that had been limited by custom. It further provided that week work traditionally lower than the new maximum was to remain unchanged. On labor services that had no traditional limit the law was silent. The next year this oversight was corrected; for disputes in this case it was provided that

> the figure accepted for this purpose shall be the highest performed by the subject in the thirty-two years before the publication of the patent . . . The fact of his performance shall be proved by the lord either by unimpeachable witnesses, or from the original register, or from some other written document. This shall be considered the true obligation and be fulfilled by the subjects without resistance, provided that it does not exceed the number of working days graciously allotted to the different categories by the Patent of June 12, 1772 and its supplement.[51]

51 *Ibid.*, I, 102-3. From the Law of October 24, 1773.

The patent also took up the question of the commutation of dues into money payments, the so-called *Reluition*.[52] Basically the law maintained that

> vassals and subjects are to fulfil their obligations with their own ploughs, vehicles and tools *in natura*. Where the lords may have accepted money payments from the subjects they are still at liberty to ask for labor services in the future if it will serve their own best interest.[53]

On the other hand, the lords on their part could not ask the peasants to pay money rent instead of labor services except " where the landowners or lords have no opportunity to make use of their subjects to perform services *in natura*." [54] In other words, commutation could only take place if the subjects asked for it and the lords consented.

In general the lords were not very anxious to have commutations take place. The value which the peasant's services possessed for them could only partly be compensated in money terms. It was difficult to find agricultural laborers, while week work solved both the problem of obtaining workers and that of compensating them. Rising prices also meant that the lord would lose by commuting services into money payments. It is almost impossible to generalize from the price data existing for Austria in that period. They are sparse, cover only a few localities, although they do include a great many commodities within those localities. The evidence seems to show that this was a period of slowly rising prices, but that no really important rise occurred until about 1800.[55] It

52 A system of conversion of services into money payments and sale of small farms to individual peasant owners had been introduced on a few crown estates in Bohemia and Styria. After its originator, Hofrath Raab, it is called Raab's System. It was to become the model for later attempts at commutation, both on crown and noble lands.

53 F. von Hauer, *op. cit.*, I, 125.

54 *Ibid.*, I, 125.

55 Alfred Francis Pribram, *Materialien zur Geschichte der Preise und Loehne in Oesterreich*, Vienna, 1938, *passim*.

therefore appears that there was no real connection between rising prices and agrarian reform in Austria. (This suggestion seems to be borne out by the fact that after 1800, when prices rose very rapidly, we find only the absence of social reform.) Although the price rise during the period of Maria Theresa appears to have been fairly unimportant, its very existence was an added reason why the lords did not wish to enter into agreements for the commutation of services.

If one reviews the clauses of the reform of labor services in Lower Austria against the background of agrarian conditions in that province, one realizes that the main merit of the reform lay in the fact that it limited and defined existing obligations. Sometimes these obligations were reduced, but nowhere were they completely abolished. In its effects the law meant peasant protection and not peasant emancipation.

The Reform of Labor Services in Styria. In Styria we find a similar story. Historically the condition of the peasants had been worse than in Lower Austria. The peasants were poorer and their lords possessed that lusty feudal spirit which constant contact with the court of Vienna had long ago eliminated in the nobles of Lower Austria. If the Styrian nobles were less disciplined, the Styrian peasants were more rebellious than those in Lower Austria. Repeatedly they sent petitions containing their grievances to Vienna. A petition of the year 1766 dealt specifically with their complaints regarding labor services. They wrote that services were demanded of them on Sundays and holidays, that they were overburdened with errands, that during harvest time they were often forced to send two or three persons for labor services. They also complained that those who missed their workday were often made to pay a fine, that frequently they were given only bread instead of the customary meal, and that the time spent in going to and from the place of work was not taken into consideration.[56]

---

[56] Anton Mell, *Die Anfänge der Bauernbefreiung im Steiermark*, Graz, 1901, p. 87.

The government consequently ordered an investigation of these grievances by the local authorities. The matter dragged on from year to year and had not yet reached any positive result when the central administration entered into negotiations with the Styrian Estates with the aim of introducing the *Robot* Patent of Lower Austria into Styria. In October 1772, it asked the provincial government to come to an agreement with the Estates, whereby the law would be adapted to Styrian needs. The government added that such a law was necessary because the subjects were overburdened with labor services. The Estates thereupon appointed a commission of inquiry, consisting of Count Ernst Herberstein, the Provost of Stainz, the Counts Wildenstein and Trautmannsdorf, and a secretary.

A month later the committee issued a report which vigorously rejected the assumption that there was any similarity between the constitution of Styria and that of Lower Austria. The main reason for the difference, they thought, lay in the fact that in Styria taxes were paid in advance by the nobles while this was not the case in Lower Austria.[57] In defense of labor services the commission pointed out that, since the nobles had once owned all the land, the services ought to be regarded either as rent paid by the peasant, or else, where he had actually bought the land, as part of the purchase contract. The commission added that, aside from laws against services on Sundays and holidays or against overburdening the peasants, there had never been any regulation of the matter by the central government for Styria. And since there was no dispute or quarrel with regard to week work in Styria now, even if in the recent census a few unfortunate cases could be found, it was incorrect to generalize and speak of an overburdening of the peasants. " There," added Mell, the main historian of Styrian peasant emancipation, " the commission spoke against its own conviction."

57 *Ibid.*, p. 89.

The committee further reported that the Estates themselves were vitally interested in keeping the peasants in "a taxable state," and that "very many" landowners had already commuted their daily and unlimited boon rights into moderate and limited ones, either in money dues or in services. This, it declared with irrefutable logic, was in "some places impossible and in others even harmful." [58] Finally the committee suggested that those who performed week work also received various privileges from the landowner in turn. It rejected the two-day services of Lower Austria, because the provisions of that patent were

> an unjustified interference by the sovereign with the age-old privileges of the Estates, and an equally unjustified degradation of the value of individual domains ... The possessors of allodial domains, counting on daily services, have acquired these estates, by purchase or heredity, for a high price, almost always with considerable debt. Through a reduction of services they lose part of their capital value and are put into an insolvent position without any fault of their own.[59]

The standing committee of the Estates accepted this report completely. The Estates were willing, however, as proof of their devotion to the Imperial house, to reduce daily boon duty to services of four days per week (208 days per year). The Imperial provincial government, in a letter to the Chancellery, advised the central government to accept the suggestions of the Estates, with the sole reservation that the peasant should not be made to work more than four days per week at any time.

The provincial government at that time consisted of such noble landowners as Count Rudolf von Wagesberg, Cajetan von Sauer, Vinzenz von Rosenberg and Gundaker von Wurmbrand. Probably a typical example of the views of these men was their opinion on unlimited labor services. This duty was, they thought, not nearly as burdensome as had usually been claimed: "For in case of hindrance the peasant can always send his serving-man or his twelve-year-old child to do the work." The landowner was not so lucky. He was responsible for the contribution of his subjects and if necessary had to advance the tax-money out of his own purse. If he could not do so he faced a fine or even total sequestration. A reduction of tax payments was no remedy for this sad situation:

> With such extreme limitations on labor services it is not very important that the payment which the landowners give on the basis of this duty is reduced. Their considerable opposition consists in the fact that it is being made impossible for them to work their farms and vineyards. Therefore their complete ruin is to be expected, especially since in many parts of the country peasants cannot be found to work such economic units.

The provincial government therefore appealed to the Empress to maintain such an equilibrium between lords and subjects that the latter " may indeed improve their economic units " but that " the landowners may not be left to utter ruin." [60]

The Chancellery, in a report to the Empress likewise found, although for different reasons, that the decree for Lower Austria was not applicable to Styria. In Lower Austria, they explained, unlimited labor services existed only infrequently and rarely had to be discharged daily. In Lower Styria both conditions were still quite prevalent. A reduction of services to three days a week would therefore make for substantial improvements in the conditions of the Styrian peasantry. At the same time it would constitute an ideal compromise between the two-day duty laid down in the decree for Lower Austria and the four-day services suggested by the Estates of Styria.

With this memorandum by the Chancellery the negotiations came to a temporary standstill. They had had little result

60 *Ibid.*, p. 92.

beyond showing the wide gulf of interest which existed between the Estates of Styria and the central government.

In the meantime the scene of agrarian interest had shifted from the German provinces to Bohemia and Moravia. In these countries, where the last major peasant revolt had taken place as late as 1688, peasant unrest was frequent. Once again the Austrian government formulated its agrarian principles with regard to the Slavic countries and then applied the finished product to one of the German provinces.

The main feature of the Bohemian patent of 1775 had been the limitation of labor services to three days a week. In 1777, the government renewed its negotiations with the Estates of Styria with the aim of introducing a similar reform. It had by this time become extremely conscious of agrarian affairs. Many of its members, moreover, including Maria Theresa herself, were frightened by the Bohemian uprising. The unrest was not confined to Bohemia. Maria Theresa wrote unhappily to her confidant, Count Mercy-Argenteau, the Austrian Ambassador at Paris:

> Not in Bohemia alone are the peasants to be feared, but also in Moravia, Styria, Austria. At our very doors, here, at home, they commit the greatest impudences. The consequences for themselves and for many innocent people are to be feared. The most daring and the most rotten have the easiest time of it.[61]

The one member of the government who did not share Maria Theresa's fears was her son and co-regent, the Emperor Joseph II. Angrily he proclaimed that the government, in which his mother was still the guiding spirit, was so inefficient that the peasants had no alternative but to revolt. Such utterances did not endear the Emperor to his mother. She even began to regard him as one of the instigators of the difficulty. Again to Mercy-Argenteau, she wrote: " The Emperor, who

61 A. v. Arneth, *op. cit.*, IX, 361.

carries his desire for popularity too far, has, on his various journeys, without making these people promises of course, spoken much too much about their freedom, both in matters of religion and from the manorial lord." [62]

The renewed negotiations had as their basis a memorandum on the *Agrarian Constitution to be Founded in the Archduchy of Styria,* written by Count Cajetan von Sauer, generally considered one of the most capable experts on the subject. The major part of the report was a long historical treatise on the rights of the manorial lord over his subjects. It concluded that " a general regulation with regard to labor services cannot be introduced into this land without the total collapse of the contracts existing between lords and subjects and of the mutual rights arising therefrom." Sauer did come out for three-day services where the peasants had hitherto been working longer, but the time between three days and longer periods of service was to be commuted into money payments.

Sauer was councillor with the provincial government for Inner Austria, and as such was an Imperial official. But his suggestions as to how this plan was to be executed clearly betrayed his interest as a great landowner. The local administration was to ask all domains for a statement on the scope of the services due to them. The lists were to be sent to the provincial government. Domains where unlimited services or week work of more than three days were still customary were to be asked to limit their demands. All these negotiations were to be kept completely secret from the peasantry, for in this fashion "the subject will be made to believe that he owes the commutation and reduction of labor services only to the kindness of the landlord and will be guided toward a greater respect and love for his master." [63]

Nothing perhaps illustrates better the struggle between the old landowning nobility and the new governmental bureaucracy

62 *Ibid.,* IX, 361.
63 A. Mell, *op. cit.,* p. 100.

than a comparison between this statement of Sauer and the
comment with which the referee on Inner Austria in the Chancellery, von Curti, presented it to the Empress for her consideration:

> The welfare of the state demands the maintenance of the sub-
> jects as the main taxpayers on whom everybody lives. There-
> fore the sovereign has not only the right, but the duty, not-
> withstanding previous pacts, contracts, judicial decisions and
> traditional customs, to obtain in this matter an adequate
> remedy which will lighten the burden of the subjects.[64]

Curti pointed out that the commutation of services of more
than three days into money payments meant no relief to the
peasantry, that by the substitution of money payments "the
same oppression would continue."[65] The only solution, he
wrote, was the abolition of all unlimited boon work and the
reduction of services to three days a week. In a peasant's fulfillment of these services only the value of his possessions was
to be taken into consideration. No attention whatever should
be paid to "former institutions or contracts."[66] In a final
report the Chancellery accepted most of Curti's suggestions
and the Empress in turn approved them.

Now the old game began anew. The government was
anxious to introduce its reform, while the Estates wanted to
prevent it at any cost. Casting around for a new device to
gain time, the latter had the secretary of their standing committee draw up a lengthy memorandum on the subject of labor
services in Styria. The tone of the document was clearly one
of "we Styrians know much more about the province than
you at Vienna," a tactic which most provinces were to use in-
creasingly against any reform by the central government. The
secretary pointed out that, of the Styrian counties, Judenburg

64 *Ibid.*, p. 105.
65 *Ibid.*, p. 105.
66 *Ibid.*, p. 107.

had limited services of less than three days per week. In Graz, Marburg, and Cilli only about thirty domains demanded more than that, while in only about ten per cent of Styria did the lords ask for unlimited or four to five day services. It was therefore unnecessary to " arouse the whole country " by a general patent.[67] The fear of the nobles that the central government would appear as the protector of the peasants seems to have been almost as great as their anxiety over financial loss.

The provincial government of Inner Austria had in the meantime drawn up another draft for a regulation of labor services. The author this time was a councillor by the name of von Ploeckhner. His report was meant to apply to the whole province and, with some exceptions, was based on the patent for Lower Austria of 1772. It received the approval of the Empress and of the Chancellery, but not of the Estates of Styria. The latter, in a dramatic gesture, called a meeting of the Assembly of the Estates. From there they called upon the Empress to show them that graciousness " which their century-long devotion deserved." " Your Majesty's love of justice praised in all the world," they declared, " is the most reliable support; on it alone rests the hope of the Estates in their distressed and just pleas." [68]

Finally the Estates, realizing that there was little they could do to prevent it, even accepted the reduction of services to three days. They only asked that there should be no regulation of anything below that. This the government was unwilling to concede and negotiations went on. The Estates sent a deputation to Vienna to plead their cause. The Governor of Styria, Count Herberstein, wrote and signed a petition to the same effect. But the government still insisted on a general regulation. On December 5, 1778, after hard labor, the *Robot* Patent for Styria was born.

67 *Ibid.*, p. 110.
68 *Ibid.*, p. 121.

It was, however, a somewhat anemic child. The law completely lacked the classification of the peasantry into whole, half, and quarter tenants, which had added so much to the precision and accuracy of the patent for Lower Austria, despite the fact that the classification had figured conspicuously in the negotiations preceding the drawing up of the measure. Neither was there any distinction made between peasants living on their own land and those living on the lord's domain.

The actual patent was short and not very specific. It provided that no peasant was to perform services for more than three days per week. If he had missed previous ones, he was to make them up, but the "cumulation [was] not to exceed four days per week." In sum, the services were not to exceed 156 days per year under any pretext whatsoever. All forms of week work, cartage, spinning, and hunting services were to be included in these 156 days. Regarding services of less than three days, all "existing customs and traditional usages" were to remain in force. The patent in effect determined only the limits of services without attempting a general regulation.

The manner in which the law was to be carried out was clarified in a fifteen-point appendix. Its first paragraph prohibited services on Sundays and holidays, except in cases of common danger. It limited the working day to eight hours from October to March and twelve from April to September, following the Bohemian rather than the Lower Austrian precedent. The provisions for bad weather, lateness, the use of tools, likewise resembled closely those of the Bohemian patent of 1775.

"All miserable, mentally or physically impaired or sixty-year-old *Inleute*" were declared entirely free from week work. So were all "single or married sons and daughters who are in the service of their parents or parents-in-law, all peasants or peasants' wives who have lost their farms on grounds other than negligence, as well as all invalids and discharged soldiers as long as they are *Inleute* and do not own a house."

The closing paragraph of the appendix dealt with spinning services which on some manors were substituted for work in the fields. The law here provided that the subjects could be asked to substitute seven hours of spinning for a day in the fields, but that they could never be held responsible for the completion of a certain prescribed task.[69]

This Styrian law was the last of the important regulations on peasant labor services in the time of Maria Theresa. For Tyrol and Vorarlberg no such rules were necessary since week work, as known in the other provinces, did not exist. The regulation for Carinthia, which had been projected, was to take place only in the time of Joseph II.

The reform of labor services was characteristic of the reform activities of Maria Theresa. She defined, set legal limits, and in some cases even reduced the obligations of the peasantry. But she made no serious attempt to abolish these obligations. She was a reformer, but only well within the framework of the existing order.

The Payment of Manorial Dues

Week work was the most pressing, the most onerous, the most burdensome, and therefore easily the most important service the peasant rendered to the Lord. It was by no means the peasant's sole payment to the landowner. Dues in kind and money were never in Austria the subject of great controversy or extensive legislation. But if the picture of the peasant's dependence on the lord is to be complete, they must be mentioned.

In the payment of the *Grundgeld* or *laudemium minor* there was, so far as can be ascertained, no great change during the reign of Maria Theresa.

The legislation on the pound money (*Pfundgeld*) was, in the main, designed to correct abuses. Theoretically there were two kinds of pound money: (1) *Totenpfundgeld* or *mortuarium*, which was paid when land changed hands after the

69 *Sammlung, op. cit.,* VIII, 219-25.

death of its owner, and (2) *Veraenderungsgeld* or *laudemium* to be given to the lord when land changed hands generally. Although previous legislation, especially the *Tractatus de Iuris Incorporabilibus* (1677) and its supplements had made it clear that only one of these dues could be demanded in a single instance, the landowners often insisted on receiving both at the same time. By an order of March 6, 1756, the Empress decreed that from then on only the *mortuarium* could be demanded should land change hands after the death of its owner. The tax was to be limited to three *Kreutzer* on the *Gulden*. This provision merely repeated a former statute which, like so much of early legislation, had not been enforced. In fact this decree was not to be enforced in its entirety either, for the Estates objected. Eventually a compromise was agreed upon. It stated that if the peasant was a true subject of the lord, his successor was to pay both *laudemium* and *mortuarium*. But where he held property only on a certain domain, and was the subject of another lord, only the *mortuarium* could be demanded.[70]

Another abuse of the lord's right to these dues sometimes occurred in instances where a holding was bequeathed to several heirs one of whom took over the economic unit and bought out the others or conversely, when it was left to the widow to administer in the name of several heirs. In both cases taxes frequently had to be paid twice. This practice the government of Maria Theresa declared to be "nonsense running counter to equity" which was to be "abolished completely and absolutely."[71]

In many cases the question arose how the value of such a holding was to be determined. Eventually it was agreed that the value accepted as basis for the payment of dues was to equal the sum set for tax purposes.[72]

70 F. v. Hauer, *op. cit.*, I, 178-81.
71 *Ibid.*, I, 183-84.
72 *Ibid.*, I, 193.

Perhaps the clearest evidence of the semi-servile state of the Austrian peasantry before the reign of Joseph II was its inability to move without the permission of the landlord. The fee which the peasant paid for being allowed to do so, the *Abfahrtgeld,* was consequently one of the major dues received by the lords. Maria Theresa apparently had no intention of abolishing these payments. On the contrary she provided that not only regular peasants, but *Inleute* as well, were to pay such dues, both on inherited property and on other peasant possessions. This was to apply even if the subject went abroad. To facilitate the immigration of peasants from the hereditary lands to the newly-acquired Galicia, however, a decree of October 23, 1773 prohibited the lords from demanding *Abfahrtgeld* from " emigrants to the Austrian part of Poland." [73]

Finally the patent of May 15, 1779 set up general standards as to what a lord could ask for his ordinary functions as overlord. For a letter of release (*Losbrief*) he was to demand no more than thirty *Kreutzer* from an ordinary peasant and should ask nothing from a poor subject, poor in this case being defined as possessing a fortune of less than fifty *Gulden*.[74] For a marriage license thirty *Kreutzer* was fixed as the maximum, the poor again being exempt from all payments. The fee for evaluation of a peasant's property was to be no more than thirty *Kreutzer,* while the subject was to pay no more than three *Kreutzer* for permission to have a look at the register of landed property. In case two peasants quarreled over a piece

73 *Sammlung, op. cit.,* VI, 625.

74 To obtain a slight idea of what fifty *Gulden* meant in Austria in the second half of the 18th century it would perhaps be useful to cite a few figures. In 1761 the yearly salary of Kaunitz, one of the best, if not the best-paid official in the monarchy was 30,000 *Gulden,* that of a teacher to the Imperial children 1,600 *Gulden*; a violinist in the court orchestra was paid ca. 400 *Gulden,* a minor government official between 300 and 900 *Gulden.* A female worker at a Graz cotton factory during the same period earned ten *Kreutzer* a day, while the government ceiling on the price of meat in Vienna was between six and eight *Kreutzer* per pound. (1 *Gulden* = 60 *Kreutzer*.)

of land, and the steward had to be called in to settle the dispute, each of the subjects was to pay one *Gulden*. From this law we also learn that the material aid which the lord always boasted of giving his subjects was not as free of charge as we have sometimes been led to believe. The government was forced to fix the price for borrowing one Lower Austrian *Metzen* (approximately one peck) of grain at one *Kreutzer* and to order that grain stocks be kept in good order and established where they did not yet exist. It also felt it necessary to set limits to the payments which a peasant could make in return for receiving lumber from the lord. Finally the law stated that if a subject had committed a crime and had to be arrested by the constable, the fee paid to the latter was to be six *Kreutzer* per mile from the place of arrest to the jail.[75]

LAND OWNERSHIP AND INHERITANCE

Ownership. Next to the complicated system of dues and services, the laws and customs pertaining to land ownership and inheritance showed most clearly the dependence of the peasant upon his lord. During the reign of Maria Theresa there were renewed attempts to prevent the so-called *Legungen* or appropriation of peasant lands by the nobles. Although this policy mainly attempted to preserve peasant land for state taxation, an idea of " peasant land to the peasantry " was also present. The definitive law in this respect was the decree of May 12, 1770, which prohibited the lord or his steward from appropriating a hereditary holding without the permission of the local government. Land that had been taken from the peasants since its registration in the *cadastre* of 1748 was to be returned to the original owner.[76] At the same time the government carried on negotiations with the estates of various provinces with the aim of facilitating the peasant's possibilities of purchasing the land he now held in usufruct only. But any

75 *Sammlung, op. cit.,* VIII, 239-49.

76 Heinrich Kretschmayr, *Maria Theresia,* Leipzig, 1938, p. 211.

definitive legislation on this point necessarily had to fail unless it forced the lord to sell such land. Such a drastic interference with the property rights of the nobles the government did not dare attempt. On the contrary it emphasized repeatedly that such steps would be left " solely to a voluntary agreement, free of all partiality and force, between lord and subjects." It did, however, make its interest in the matter clear by adding that a register of such " tranferred lands [was] to be sent to court annually." [77]

In Carinthia the government actually did take the bold step of abolishing the *Freistiftlichkeit* (free disposal of peasant property by the lord) and thus secured legal hereditary rights for the peasant. It declared that this step had been absolutely necessary. Otherwise the peasant could never be certain whether, after his death, his family would enjoy the improvements he had made on his farm. This uncertainty seemed to the government " the most natural, yes the only reason, why agriculture has been carried on in this province in so dilatory a fashion that irreparable harm has been done to the public welfare." [78]

Size of agricultural holdings. Together with these efforts to provide the peasant with a secure succession to his farm, the state concerned itself with the problem of keeping the holding together. The problem of free divisibility versus regulated succession was one of the questions much discussed during the eighteenth century. Closely allied to it was the problem as to what the ideal size of an economic unit should be to achieve maximum efficiency in production. It remained for the men of the nineteenth century to witness the full flowering of this discussion. But the beginnings of it are clearly found in the writings of the eighteenth-century cameralists. At that time small units were considered most desirable. This fitted in well with the eighteenth century attitude that ownership

77 *Sammlung, op. cit.*, VII, 20.
78 *Ibid.*, VI, 542-48.

alone would make for zeal and industry in cultivation, as well
as with the idea of intensive agriculture then coming to the
fore. Justi, for instance, thought that thirty *Morgen* [79] of 180
Rhenish quarter sections each, would be " adequate and even
less [land would be] sufficient ", for " the less land the common
people have, the better they seek to cultivate and use it. " [80]

But while Justi also advocated that a peasant should be able
to divide his farm freely, the government was opposed to
such a policy. It feared that continued division would decrease
the strength of the economic unit and therefore detract from the
livelihood of the peasantry. It prohibited the parcelling out of
land into very small farms and the division of large holdings
into more than four parts. No division of any kind was to
take place " without the consent of the lord in agreement with
the provinical government." [81] A year later a government
order pursuing the same aim prohibited the separate sale of
any land not contiguous to the farmhouse but traditionally
belonging to it (*Hausueberlandesgrund*).[82]

The Common Pasture. Another way to add to peasant land
under cultivation was to enclose the common pasture and to
divide the land among the peasants. The priniciples for this
action were laid down in a law of March 24, 1770. A part of
the common pasture was to be allocated to each peasant who
had hitherto made use of it. He was free to "hedge it in, enclose
it," or otherwise preserve it against game damage. He also
acquired legal ownership as soon as he had entered his new
possession " in the register of landed property . . . as
an indivisible and non-salable piece of land, with the remark

79 The extent of the *Morgen* differed in various regions of Germany. It
generally, however, varied between 25 and 30 ares, that is, between a
little over ½ and about ¾ acres.

80 Else Cronbach, "Das Landwirtschaftliche Betriebsproblem," *Studien
zur Sozial- Wirtschafts- und Verwaltungsgeschichte*, Vienna, 1907, p. 27.

81 *Sammlung, op. cit.*, VII, 20.

82 *Ibid.*, VI, 540.

that it stemmed from the division of the common pasture."
The law concluded by categorically declaring all previous agreements between lords and subjects, " if they were concluded for
a fee higher than that of the patent," null and void.[83]

The government, which was opposed to the sale of all
peasant land, vigorously opposed any 'sale of land obtained
from the division of the common pasture. Such land could
be disposed of only if the peasant could prove that he was
well provided with meadows and acres, and that the pasture
land was too far from his other holdings to be useful to him.
Even then he had to obtain special permission from his overlord.[84]

The division of the pasture did not run smoothly. In the
government's opinion the landlords were responsible for most
of the difficulties. In January 1780, ten years after the publication of the original decree, the government was still asking
that all pasture land be divided within three months. Proof
of the distribution or statements why it had not taken place
had to be sent to the local administration. In case of neglect
the provincial government was to enforce the law at the expense of the lord.[85]

Division of Peasant Property. While in the case of the distribution of the common pasture the nobles were the obstruct-
ing party they, in contrast to the government, were quite
favorable to the division of peasant property. Such at least is
the contention of Archduke Otto in his study on the law and
customs of peasant inheritance in Austria in which he main-
tains that, while the nobles had nothing to lose from the split-
ting up of land if their dues were not attacked, they would
gain new revenue from the act of division itself.[86]

83 *Ibid.*, VI, 179-81.

84 *Ibid.*, VI, 580.

85 *Ibid.*, VIII, 400.

86 Otto, Archduke of Austria, *Coutumes et Droits Successoraux de la
Classe Paysanne et L'Indivision des Proprietées Rurales en Autriche,*
Vienna, 1935, p. 13.

The debate of divisibility versus regulated succession did not end with the measures discussed in the previous pages. Where Maria Theresa had only made a beginning, her son was to continue with determination and vigor.

TOWARDS A HAPPIER, HEALTHIER, AND MORE MANAGEABLE PEASANTRY

If the Austrian peasantry was to become the stable and healthy peasantry which the government of Maria Theresa visualized, a formal dissolution of the landowner-peasant relationship was not enough. It was also necessary to improve the health, welfare and material environment of the rural population. Only in that fashion could the peasant, oppressed in so many ways, become really emancipated, really human, and at the same time a useful instrument of the state.

Size of Population. The fact that such solicitude would increase the size of the population was the motivation for many of the government's actions. This was true of the formal attempt to dissolve the landowner-peasant relationship. It was also true of other measures taken for the welfare of the peasantry.

The basic principles of this population policy were very simple. The lords, upon whose permission all peasant marriages depended, were frequently remonstrated to give such permissions willingly. The marriage of girls to persons living outside the manor was also advocated. "The marriage between female subjects and soldiers," read a resolution dated Graz, December 27, 1776, "shall not be hindered but facilitated by all means." Likewise illegitimate children born to peasant girls were not to be brought to Vienna, "and abandoned," but were to be taken care of by the manorial lord.[87] Another administrative order warned peasant women and rural housewives "to keep a watchful eye on the pregnancies of their serving-folk,"[88] To prevent any decrease in the popu-

87 *Sammlung, op. cit.,* III, 190.
88 *Ibid.,* V, 242-43.

lation it was decreed that, " in order to prevent emigration, no certificate of baptism shall, without the permission of the manorial lord, be issued to any subject staying in a foreign land.[89]

The most effective way of keeping check on the movement of population was a regular census, a procedure which under the pretty name of " description of souls " was introduced into Austria in 1753. At first it took place every three years, but after 1762 annually.

The census was opposed both by the nobles and the Church. The former were afraid that census-takers would see the living conditions of their peasants. The latter seem to have been mindful of the biblical injunction against the counting of heads and apparently also feared that the great emphasis on the growth of the population would only lead to further agitation against monasticism.[90] In Austria, as in most mercantilist countries, the state and most economic thinkers were strongly opposed to celibacy. They advocated instead that an increase in the population should be encouraged by all means, and were in turn accused of holding a " recruiting sergeant theory of population."

Conscription. It is quite logical that few plans for the welfare of the peasantry omitted the canon-fodder aspect in a century in which eight major wars were fought. It is also obvious that many of the country boys subject to conscription looked for ways and means of avoiding it. Repeatedly the government was forced to pass laws prohibiting prospective recruits from pulling out their teeth or otherwise mutilating themselves.[91]

Even the eighteenth-century state realized the importance of food production as the basis for maintaining an efficient

89 *Ibid.,* V, 239.

90 Karl Uhlirz, *Handbuch der Geschichte Oesterreichs und seiner Nachbarländer Ungarn und Boehmen,* Graz, 1927, II, 350.

91 For instance the Rescript of February 21, 1756, *Sammlung, op. cit.,* III, 315.

army, and frequently released from military service [92] peasants who had inherited or otherwise obtained land. It took care, however, that such relief did not become an easy exit from the army and usually provided that nobody could be released until the situation had been thoroughly investigated by the regiment.[93]

Public Order. An increase in the size of the population would profit the government little unless it could establish a firm grip over its actions and thoughts. All the traditions of the eighteenth-century peasantry were opposed to such control. But, unless it could be established, legislation of any kind, even the measures directed toward the emancipation of the peasantry, would fall on barren ground.

If the laws of the central government were to be enforced, it was necessary to prevent the peasants from taking the law into their own hands. In concrete terms this meant that it was necessary to take their arms away from them. One of the first laws issued by Maria Theresa with regard to the peasantry was directed towards that end.

> No peasant or serving man shall, under any pretext whatever, keep fire-arms in his house. He shall neither buy them nor dare acquire them in any other fashion. All fire-arms are to be delivered to the manorial lord voluntarily. The subjects shall also refrain from buying gunpowder or lead, either personally or through others. Over all this the manorial officials are to keep the most thorough control.[94]

Anti-centralist historians like Beidtel [95] have raised a great hue and cry over this decree claiming that it deprived the

92 Decree of February 12, 1774, and Rescript of April 19, 1771. *Ibid.*, VII, 21 and VI, 340.

93 *Ibid.*, VII, 21.

94 *Ibid.*, I, 5-6.

95 Ignaz Beidtel, *Geschichte der Oesterreichischen Staatsverwaltung*, Innsbruck, 1889, is among historians, the most outspoken critic of the centralizing reforms of Maria Theresa and Joseph II.

people of their ancient liberties. The argument seems beside
the point. There was no real liberty in eighteenth-century Austria, even for a peasant who owned a gun. The most that
could be hoped for was a certain degree of economic stability
and security, emancipation of the peasants and equality before
the law. But in the face of the existing disorder even these
objectives could not be achieved. The proponents of the
mercantilist state realized clearly that before making their
state healthy, wealthy, and strong, they had first to make it
orderly.

The laws passed for this purpose often seem in their details
unwarranted, crude, and sometimes even downright ridiculous.
Thus an old law against vagabonds was revived with the
provision that the order for searches should be kept secret
and communicated only orally to the officials concerned and
that, immediately before the search, all "ways, paths and
other places of refuge shall be occupied so that none can
escape." Then the "caught scum" were to be asked for their
"place of birth, age, status, the place of their stay, the amount
of alms collected or of money or goods smuggled or stolen."
Eventually these "bands of thieves and gypsies" were to be
taken care of with the assistance of the military. For this purpose the government ordered that "each official must co-
operate with united effort [sic!] if he does not wish to incur
punishment." In case one of the "scum" refused to give the
desired information, torture was authorized. For the particular benefit of agriculture it was ordered that "peasants and
subjects who had lost their property" were to be sent back
to where they came from.[96]

Aside from the somewhat merciless attitude towards vagabonds, the most striking provision of this law would seem
to be the paragraph in which the government threatened its
own officials with punishment, if they did not execute the decrees it promulgated. How well these warnings worked we do

96 Sammlung, op. cit., I, 136-42.

not know. That they could not have been overly effective is seen by the fact that six years later the government still decreed that gypsies who had entered the country illegally were " to be taken care of and eliminated." [97] In the same year it also decided that all vagabonds, religious and secular hermits were to be arrested.[98] This provision was probably based on the frequent attempts of vagabonds to disguise themselves as monks, a ruse against which the government warned its officials by a law of August 29, 1761.[99] The final word on the subject came in a decree of March 3, 1766, which summarily stated that vagabonds should be prevented from marrying.[100] If the government thought that, by this quasi-Malthusian device, it would prevent the birth of baby-vagabonds, its reasoning was a bit naive.

Into this same category of creating order fall the attemps to regulate the social and personal life of the peasantry, or rather, to do away with what the government considered its excesses and abuses. Events which were prone to create disorders and disturbances were rigidly circumscribed and if possible abolished altogether. On May 1, 1753 for instance, a decree was passed in Lower Austria with the expressed purpose of " abolishing excessive gaity among the young peasant folk."

> For the abolition of excessive gaiety and the sinful life, especially among the young peasant folk, which stem partly from unrestrained nightly meetings, partly from dances held until late into the night, and partly also from the immodest garments worn by some women in parts of this country, it is ordered that these late meetings cease completely, and that dances shall not last later than nine o'clock in winter and ten o'clock in summer.

97 *Ibid.*, III, 340.
98 *Ibid.*, III, 341.
99 *Ibid.*, VI, 73.
100 *Ibid.*, V, 27.

In its final paragraph the law threatened to punish all concerned, innkeepers, officials, tailors, as well as the young people themselves, if they did not comply with its provisions.[101]

While this act was pervaded by the strict morality of Maria Theresa, a decree of the following year betrayed more fully the government's fear of rural disturbances. From its preamble we learn that indecent songs were being sung at funerals and also that " here and there peasants, who fancy themselves capable of this, deliver complete funeral orations, with admixture of various scriptural texts and other teachings not suitable for edification in the death house or the church." To make such incidents impossible it was provided that, in the future, funeral songs must be approved by village priests and speeches confined " to the bare account of the life of the deceased." [102]

In all this the effort to prevent agitation and disorder was obvious. In 1769 church meals were prohibited [103] and in 1771 wedding and *primitia* meals reduced from three days to one.[104] The next year saw the closing of all taverns on Sundays until four o'clock in the afternoon.[105]

Although much of this legislation may appear to have been an unnnecessary and petty interference with the personal lives of the people, it must also be given credit for destroying much that was cruel and superstitious in rural life. The government prohibited the " old peasant custom " of burying people alive at the carnival.[106] It forbade the peasants to fasten roots, herbs, and flowers at doors and windows to keep away evil spirits,[107] or to carry off glowing branches from the consecrated wood on

101 *Ibid.*, II, 146-49.
102 *Ibid.*, II, 400.
103 *Ibid.*, V, 443.
104 *Ibid.*, VI, 363.
105 *Ibid.*, VI, 436.
106 *Ibid.*, VI, 239.
107 *Ibid.*, VIII, 391.

Easter Sundays.[108] Typical in connection with the government's fight against superstitious practices is the Edict on Almanacs, usually ascribed to Maria Theresa's own hand. In it she expresses approval of two kinds of almanacs, one " for clever people ", the other, however,

> for the common people in which all fast and feast days, rise and setting of the sun, as well as quarters and eclipses shall be recorded. Not, however, the foolish observations about bleeding, cupping, swallowing things, cutting of hair, nails, etc., or signs of fortunate and unfortunate days. All these things are to be prohibited in all lands in the future . . . The almanacs are generally read, often the only book read in rural areas, and in many of them there are said to be insipid, also coarse and useless, stories which are to be dispensed with completely.[109]

Rural Education. Where the government destroyed, it also attempted to create. It is perhaps no accident that, along with this fight against disorder and superstitious practices, we find the beginnings of compulsory elementary education in Austria. The cause and effect relationship in this connection should not be overemphasized. We have no proof that Maria Theresa or her advisers thought of the new school system as a formidable weapon of popular enlightenment. But they did believe that a little education would create a more manageable and " virtuous " class of subjects. As Kaunitz wrote in a memorandum to Maria Theresa:

> As the prince needs the heads, as well as the arms and purses of his subjects, and as his projects, his designs, his views and his laws cannot be put into practice without instruments proper to their execution, nothing is more important than to have, or to be able to find, such instruments, and nothing is more necessary in forming them than education . . . The

108 *Ibid.*, VIII, 236.
109 E. Guglia, *op. cit.*, I, 90-1.

strength of the state depends on the good fortune of having virtuous citizens. Education can make them in all the climates of the world.[110].

Turning to the education of the peasantry in particular, Kaunitz continued: " All citizens are either laborers, burghers or noblemen. The first of these classes is the least instructed, perhaps because it comprises the greatest number of human beings or perhaps because it lacks means and faculties. At any rate it demands the greatest care and instruction."[111]

To give the peasantry this " greatest care and instruction " three aspects of education were to be emphasized: religion, morality, and practical training. The meaning of religious education was self-evident. Moral education, on the other hand, had to be defined more clearly. It was " to teach that class of men a morality in conformity with their station " in life:

> One must give them a horror of theft, lying, drunkenness, ingratitude, and all the vices that the laws do not punish ... One must inspire them with a love of the Prince as their common father and of their country as the mother who nurses them, with submission to their station in society, with fidelity and obedience. One must finally give them the highest idea of the reward which, in this world or the next, awaits those who make the supreme sacrifice in the service of their sovereign.[112]

In the realm of practical training the Chancellor advocated that peasant children be given " elementary lessons and notions of rural economy, agriculture, feeding and maintenance of animals, veterinary arts, and all the activities most necessary to the country." [113]

110 Adolf Beer (ed.), " Denkschriften des Fuersten Kaunitz," *Archiv fuer Oesterreichische Geschichte*, Vienna, 1872, XLVIII, 100.

111 *Ibid.*, p. 101.

112 *Ibid.*, p. 102.

113 *Ibid.*, p. 103.

The section on rural education in the famous Patent on Education of 1774 follows closely the plan Kaunitz had outlined. Country boys and girls were to attend school from their sixth to their thirteenth year. Those between the ages of six and eight were to go from Easter to Michelmas except for three weeks during harvest time, and were to stay at home in the winter. The older children, those between the ages of nine and thirteen, were to attend school from Christmas to the end of March, since they had to help their elders in the summer. The law made a special point of explaining that the service of orphans on the manor should not prevent them from attending classes.

The subjects to be studied in the " Common German Schools " were first of all religion, as the Chancellor had suggested, followed by the alphabet and arithmetic, which he had neglected to mention. The education was completed by a course in " guidance towards uprightness and economy suitable for country-folk." [114]

Health and Sanitation. Elementary education of children was clearly not enough to teach the Austrian peasantry " rural economy, agriculture, feeding and maintenance of animals, veterinary arts, and all the activities most necessary to the country." The government supplemented this education by a barrage of circulars and government orders on rural health and sanitation.

One very important innovation was that in the future neither doctors nor pharmacists were to practice if they had not studied at an Austrian university and passed a final examination.[115] The standards of health were to be further improved by laws warning against specific dangers of illness. The use of arsenic in the making of cheese was prohibited " on pain of fine and corporal punishment." [116] Another circular warned that a cer-

114 *Sammlung, op. cit.,* VII, 124-27.

115 *Ibid.,* VIII, 9.

116 *Ibid.,* VIII, 6.

tain weed (*Thornkraut*), " when eaten in bread, causes people violent pain, contraction of joints and limbs, paralysis, dullness in the head, and finally death in convulsions." [117]

The concern for human illness was, however, by no means as great as that for animal disease. Cattle plagues were frequent, widespread, and apparently extremely contagious. The Austrian code of laws for the years from 1740 to 1780 is interspersed at the rate of about one every two months, and often more than that, with suggestions as to what could be used as remedies against cattle plague. The cures ranged from such inoffensive, and probably ineffective, medicines as different kinds of boiled leaves to concoctions whose main ingredients were masculine urine and pigeon excretae.[118] The culmination, although by no means the end of these instructions, was a recommendation of November 2, 1762. It laid down in the greatest details all rules to be observed in the treatment of stricken animals.[119] In another instruction one half of a fresh herring every second day was suggested as a preventive measure.[120] In yet another effort to prevent infections from spreading the law of December 11, 1762, ordered that any peasant directly or indirectly associated with rinderpest should not be called for services; " after being purified and having changed clothes ", such peasants were to be kept in clean surroundings for eight days.

Skinners. For similar reasons skinners were forbidden to sell the meat or tongues of animals which had died a natural death. Lords and village authorities were asked to visit skinners frequently and without warning, to make certain that the government's command was obeyed.[121]

117 *Ibid.*, VIII, 515-16.
118 *Ibid.*, II, 401.
119 *Ibid.*, IV, 120.
120 *Ibid.*, III, 454.
121 *Ibid.*, II, 188.

During periods of cattle illness, the skinner became a most important member of the community. Apparently the transactions in which he was involved were so frequent that the government felt it necessary to put a ceiling on the prices that he could ask for his services.[122]

Sometimes when animal mortality became particularly high there were not enough skinners to take care of the dead cattle. Therefore a law of December 17, 1773 provided that during a rinderpest epidemic, " when skinners are unable to bury the great number of dead cattle, the peasants can take over that function without damaging their honor." [123] The last sentence of the law is interesting in that it shows again the pariah-like role of the skinner in the community. Only by divorcing himself completely from his former profession could an ex-skinner become an honorable man. At least he became such in the eyes of the law. The same was by no means true for the community in which he lived. By a decree of October 17, 1753, the government warned that " skinners, knackers, and dog-catchers shall, as soon as they have laid down their profession, by no means be considered as dishonorable, neither they nor their children." Consequently they were allowed to become shepherds or peasants, to take up various rural professions, and even to buy land.[124] Almost twenty years later another decree confirmed the provisions of the law of 1753, with regard to these " most unfortunate people," but added that sons of skinners, who had practiced their father's profession at any time, had to obtain an official legitimization from the government to become " honorable." [125]

Agricultural Laborers. In mentioning the outcasts of an eighteenth-century rural community one should not forget

122 *Ibid.,* V, 350-52.

123 *Ibid.,* VI, 625. The law apparently did not work for it was repealed on May 31, 1777 in Austria and on June 30 of the same year in Styria.

124 *Ibid.,* II, 247.

125 *Ibid.,* VI, 478-9.

the agricultural laborers, servants to the richer peasants, who profited from few of the reforms discussed in this chapter. For the most part the measures were not designed for their benefit. Peasant emancipation in Austria had its origin in an attempt at a new pattern of taxation and was essentially bound up with whatever property a peasant might hold. For those who held no property there could consequently be little relief. Neither, it seems, did the charity of the Empress extend that far down the scale:

> We observe, not without displeasure, what great torment, vexation and damage the peasant has to endure from his serving-folk, and how the insolence of these people has already grown so great that they lay down the law to the master of the house, leave their service at their good pleasure, and are not abashed to indulge their lewd desires so far that much scandal arises therefrom and the good discipline, on which Christian life is chiefly based, is wholly broken down.[126]

Efforts to Improve the Material Environment

Reforestation. Even agricultural laborers were to benefit by the measures with which the government sought to improve the material environment of the eighteenth-century peasantry.

One problem which affected the rural population greatly, which seemed to put a definite check on the expansion of arable land and which even threatened to become disastrous to the whole society, was the shortage of wood. This was a phenomenon recognized all over eighteenth-century Europe. In Austria the shortage was viewed with fear and trembling. We, in an age of rapid mechanical invention can hardly understand how deep this anxiety really was. Wood to the men of the eighteenth century meant warmth and it meant shelter. Without it the very existence of man was in the balance. The cameralist Justi, who worried less about it than a great many others, wrote:

126 C. A. Macartnay, *The Social Revolution in Austria*, Cambridge, 1926, p. 192.

I do not claim, as some in exaggerated patriotic warning have done, that the wood shortage can rise to such a degree that the existence of man is in the balance ... It is certain, however, that if the shortage of wood continues to rise at the present rate, it will make for a very sad situation. It is easy to see that an ever-increasing price of wood will necessitate the closing of mines, factories, and manufacturing establishments, because of lack of wood.[127]

Justi thought that the effects of such a development on the peasantry would be disastrous:

If the rural population will not have, or is unable to pay for wood, they will be forced to burn their straw. Consequently they will have little fertilizer for their acres, and the acres themselves will bear little fruit. And when, as a result of the shortage of wood, most manufacturing establishments and factories will have to close, the products of agriculture will find no market, and agriculture itself and all food production will be ruined.[128]

As means of avoiding such a situation, means which now seem pathetically inadequate, Justi suggested the stabilization of the price of wood, prohibition of its export, restriction of its consumption and the use of peat and coal. He warned the peasantry to be very careful about existing forests, and attempted to encourage them to start new ones. He urged the planting of saplings on any spot that could possibly be used for the purpose, the banks of rivers and brooks, the edges of the public highway, the common pasture. He also believed that luxury ought to be curtailed, large buildings discouraged, the number of fireplaces in a home restricted, and more than one home per family prohibited.[129]

127 Johann Heinrich Gottlieb von Justi, *Die Grundfeste zu der Macht und Glueckseligkeit der Staaten*, Koenigsberg, 1760, p. 89.

128 *Ibid.*, p. 90.

129 *Ibid.*, pp. 91-8.

The Austrian government did not follow the more extreme of these suggestions. It did, however, take various measures which were in line with Justi's train of thought.

Peasants were forbidden to gather wood in the forest except to meet their personal needs.[130] All pasture land which had not been registered in the *cadastre* of 1748, and which was subsequently discovered, was thrown open for the planting of trees. All land which had been registered as forest land, but had been used for other purposes, was to be reforested after two years.[131]

These laws were supplemented by a regulation of April 5, 1754, which stated that, except in Alpine regions, wood could be cut from December to February only. No subject could do so, moreover, either in his own forests, or in those belonging to the community, without the permission of the lord,[132] a provision which was reiterated by a resolution of February 11, 1769.[133] The government also complained that trees were being cut down in a wasteful manner, and that little care was taken to provide new ones immediately. Eventually, as was its wont in cases of this nature, it issued the customary recommendation. This time it contained fifteen pages of detailed instructions suggesting remedies for the situation. Apparently this instruction did not suffice, for the next year new regulations were issued.

Enforcement of these regulations depended mainly on local appointees: the forester and his helpers. After 1756 the latter were subjected to a rather rigorous examination before being allowed to exercise their vocation. The instruction sent to foresters by the government contained thirty pages of questions and answers, discussing differences between the various kinds of trees, their seed, planting, growth, quality and use of the

130 *Sammlung, op. cit.*, I, 44.

131 *Ibid.*, I, 368.

132 *Ibid.*, II, 399.

133 *Ibid.*, III, 564-65.

wood. It also covered other problems of rural economy; for instance, why pigs should not be allowed to run around in the forest.[134]

While in the foregoing regulations the government tried to insure the continued growth of the country's forests, it also attempted to restrict the use of wood by decreeing that neither the lower parts of houses nor " stables, barns, sheds, and similar buildings " should be built of wood.[135] Living hedges were to replace wooden fences and streets were to be covered with stone.[136]

Fire Protection. While the Austrian government and intellectuals like Justi were very much concerned about the shortage of wood, the peasants were indifferent to it. The threat seemed far away and not very concrete. Fire-hazards, on the other hand, were an ever-present threat. The peasants themselves were very active in fighting this danger, and rural fire protection remained for a long time a matter of local agreement rather than of governmental policy.

We find the roots of this rural protection in the peasant assurance (insurance) funds (*Bauernassuranzkassen*), the first of which, according to Leimdoerfer, was established in Kremsmuenster in 1710. Membership in such a society was locally limited and usually formed by the subjects on a single manor. Either, as in the Herrschaft of Puernstein in Upper Austria, the peasants took up a collection when the need for help arose, or else there was, as on the domain of the Monastery of Kremsmuenster, a permanent fund into which each member of the community paid a fixed amount annually. The assistance to the unfortunate peasant could take two main forms. A good example is the community of Spital on the Phyrn in Upper Austria where both forms of protection were to be found. First, on the demand of the elders of the com-

134 *Ibid.*, III, 269-307.
135 *Ibid.*, VII, 157.
136 *Ibid.*, II, 179.

munity, the victim was to be freed from dues and services to the manorial lord for three years. Futhermore he was given money from the fund with which to rebuild his house.[137] State help in cases of fire also existed in Theresa's Austria, but was, in the main, restricted to the Slavic provinces, except that the Law of March 31, 1777, guaranteed compensation for fire and water damages to the population of Lower Austria. In Carinthia also there existed a fund, the interest of which was to take care of such misfortunes. But, since this interest only amounted to 2,933 *Gulden* annually, it was, according to. Leimdoerfer's estimate, only about enough to take care of the damage done by hail in that province every year.[138]

In Tyrol the Estates flatly refused a suggestion by the central government to introduce general fire insurance. Tyrol was the only Austrian province where the peasantry, by virtue of its seat in the Estates, had a say in the matter. Its representatives seem to have concurred fully with the prevailing opinion. Basically they seem to have distrusted the whole scheme, fearing that it was only another governmental device to wring money from an already overburdened population. This, at least, would explain their repeated references to the poverty of the country which, exhausted by the war (1763), would be unable to bear new taxes. But technical reasons were also presented. The representatives of the Upper and Lower Inn Valley pointed out that the peasants would hardly profit by entering a general society. In the country, they argued, the houses lay far apart, and fires were relatively rare, while in the cities one fire could spread to a whole district. They thought that, as things would probably work out, the peasantry would have to pay far more than its relative share.[139] In the

---

137 Max Leimdoerfer, "Brandschadenversicherung in Oesterreich," *Studien zur Sozial- Wirtschafts- und Verwaltungsgeschichte*, Vienna, 1905, pp. 8-11.

138 *Ibid.*, p. 32.

139 *Ibid.*, pp. 54-5.

main, therefore, fire protection in eighteenth-century Austria remained a matter between the lord and his subjects, or sometimes for the subjects alone.

Hunting Rights. In all countries of the old regime hunting privileges constituted one of the surest marks of nobility. In France there was severe criticism of these rights. In Austria the legitimacy of the privilege was not questioned, but the fact that it did exist gave rise to many questions and problems.

Poaching was common. Heavy penalities were put on this practice, but their effect was slight. Unfortunately also, the enforcement of these penalties sometimes led to disastrous results. Such a possibility was implied in a law of July 21, 1756, which provided that poachers ought to be warned before being shot.[140] The government, moreover, seems to have been a bit at a loss as to what to do with a poacher once he had been caught and jailed: " One matter is very close to my heart," wrote Maria Theresa to Count Seilern, the Governor of Lower Austria, "he and the Vice-governor may reflect whether, since so many have been sent to jail for poaching, one could not this time, when everything is quiet, give an amnesty for all those who have been arrested, or perhaps only for some." [141]

But there was another aspect to the question, the damage caused by game to the peasant's fields and garden. The government's attitude in this respect was unequivocal. The law of September 18, 1766 stated categorically and without qualification that the peasants should be fully compensated for all such damages.[142] To make this compensation " surer and more reliable " it was ordered that in case of complaint there should be an immediate inquiry. The investigation was to be undertaken by a commission of two, one of whom was to be chosen by the landlord, the other by the subject. The commission was to assess the damage and the estimated compensation was

140 *Sammlung, op cit.,* V, 75.

141 A. v. Arneth, *op. cit.,* V, 366.

142 *Sammlung, op. cit.,* V, 129.

to be paid immediately. If the lord refused to send a representative, or else defaulted, the peasants were to be free to send their own estimators and to press their claim with the assistance of a government lawyer.[143]

Agricultural Improvements. The measures which we have discussed so far under the heading of improving the material environment of the rural population were in the main preventive. They were directed against the shortage of wood, against fire hazards, against damage caused by game. But there were also positive efforts, efforts that had their roots both in the mercantilist tradition and in that spirit of agrarian innovation which, developed and publicized in the Britain of the Agricultural Revolution, soon found its way to enlightened governments and individuals on the Continent of Europe.

The darling of the mercantilists, the silkworm, was still in the forefront. A resolution of August 1763, suggested that individual lords and convents cultivate mulberry trees in their gardens, promising free seed and compensation if this were done.[144] An administrative order of July 30, 1765, renewed the appeal and specifically asked that priests set a good example.[145] The matter was of such importance that the Austrian government employed Justi, already a well-known publicist, to write a little theoretical treatise, called *A Clear Lesson in the Cultivation of Silkworms and the Production of Silk for the Imperial Royal Hereditary Lands.*[146] Publishing these little instructions became a frequent device by which the government hoped to influence agricultural methods. Pamphlets appeared on a variety of subjects, on *How to Produce Fine Wool, How to Plant Pumpkins which in View of the Rising Price of Grain Can Serve as Food for the Poor.*

143 *Ibid.*, VIII, 216-17.

144 *Ibid.*, IV, 174-5.

145 *Ibid.*, IV, 506.

146 J. H. G. von Justi, *Neue Wahrheiten zum Vorteil der Naturkunde und des Gesellschaftlichen Lebens der Menschen*, Leipzig, 1754, pp. 22-37.

Sometimes these lessons became documents of profound learning and lyrical pathos. The author of the *Dissertation on the Usefulness of Raising Sheep in Styria* began by pointing out that sheep-raising was the first occupation of our ancestors from which " mighty peoples and empires had developed." He then went on to paint the following idyllic picture of the uses of sheep.

> The lamb or sheep is the symbol of gentleness, patience and concord. What is more vulnerable to the uncertain chance happenings of the elements than a peasant farm which lies unprotectedly beneath them? Who then needs gentleness, patience and concord more than the peasant and the members of his family Shall he not then, in order to have so necessary a symbol before his eyes at all times, give the sheep also a place in his home?

But that was not all. As a typical child of the eighteenth century the author knew that there was a pre-established harmony between the good and the useful. " In the whole animal kingdom," he went on, " there is not a single animal of which the master of the house can make as much use as he can of sheep." Their produce, he pointed out, could be used to make " blankets, stockings, hats, fur coats, leather, parchment, glue, milk, butter, cheese. Their intestines could be made into pleasant sounding strings, their hoofs into fertilizer, their tallow into candles." The manure of the sheep would give acres a wondrous growth and allow them to multiply their fertility four or five times without effort. Even the sheep's footprints would " make the grain rise and multiply itself." [147]

As these examples may have shown, the treatises were not always necessarily the most practical instructions in helping those who wished to improve their produce or livestock. Perhaps somewhat more effective was the establishment of plant and animal stations, like the aviary for bee culture in

147 *Sammlung, op. cit.,* VIII, 250-305.

the garden of the Belvedere at Vienna,[148] or the sheep farm at Merkopail whence those "nobler beasts" were to be distributed throughout various parts of the hereditary lands. Those who received the animals were to send samples of wool to Merkopail each year to indicate what progress had been made in breeding.[149]

Agricultural Societies. The reign of Maria Theresa also witnessed a flourishing growth of agricultural societies in Austria. In most provinces such groups had been established on the initiative of the inhabitants themselves. In 1769, however, they were made compulsory for all provinces.[150] The government gave them a great deal of support, encouraging them by grants and prizes. It saw in these societies agencies for the promotion of more scientific and efficient agricultural methods. Clearly the emancipation of the Austrian peasant depended not alone on a formal independence from his former master. A new mode of agriculture had to be found by which the lord would no longer depend solely upon the labor of his subjects, and which in turn would provide the peasants with the means of shaping their new independence into a happier and more prosperous life.

RETROSPECT

In retrospect the reforms of Maria Theresa suggest a pattern which in reality they did not possess. The sources of peasant emancipation in Austria came from many quarters. Probably the least important motive was an explicit desire to emancipate the peasants. We have attempted to show how incidental to agrarian reform were the initial measures: a more efficient system of taxation, a tighter Imperial administration. But in order to carry them out the Empress and her advisors had to realize the one cardinal fact in Austrian

148 *Ibid.,* VII, 204-8.
149 *Ibid.,* VII, 191 and VII, 217.
150 A. von Arneth, *op. cit.,* IX, 385.

life, namely that the peasantry formed the majority of the population. No matter where the government started, it was always forced to deal with the peasantry. An increase in direct taxes brought with it an adjustment of the peasant's dues and services. A desire to increase the general prosperity of the country meant that agrarian production had to be stimulated. A more efficient Imperial administration was impossible without control over the majority of the subjects, involving, inevitably, a reduction of the lords' power. But this better administration had to be financed. An increased tax burden demanded, in the short run, an increase in direct taxes and, in the long run, a prosperous country. These goals could hardly be achieved without a further adjustment of dues and services, a further stimulus to agrarian production. Whatever governmental problem was approached, somewhere along the road its solution seemed to call for agrarian reform. Neither Maria Theresa nor her advisers, with few exceptions, were self-conscious reformers. The beginnings of peasant emancipation in Austria had practically no ideological basis. They represented in no sense an attempt to overthrow an old order or to create a new one.

But the sum of the piecemeal innovations formed a pattern which could be used for a thoroughgoing reform program. Maria Theresa had laid the foundations upon which peasant emancipation could be carried out. But the philosophy and the will were lacking. Her successor, Joseph II, was to provide both.

CHAPTER III

A DECADE OF REVOLUTION

JOSEPH II has aroused much historical controversy. Had he deliberately set out to leave behind him a memory which would antagonize most major interest groups in nineteenth century politics, both on the conservative and on the liberal side, he could not have succeeded more thoroughly. Democrats disliked his absolutism, believers his anti-clericalism; nationalists were offended by his cosmopolitanism, and non-German elements of the Habsburg Empire by his Germanization policy which they thought, or claimed to think, was German nationalism. Most of all, perhaps, his uncompromising rationalism was diametrically opposed to the dominant attitudes of the nineteenth century.

Despite these handicaps, Joseph II, the " People's Emperor," became to many a legendary figure. Even those who disliked him most, have rarely denied the merit of his attempt to emancipate the peasants. But while few have quarrelled with the principle, many have objected to the manner of its execution. They have claimed that the reform was but a slavish and unimaginative application of the thought of the Enlightenment, that it had little root in reality and was therefore bound to fail. A closer examination of the Emperor's thought and actions does not, it would seem, bear out this contention.

THE POLITICAL THOUGHT OF JOSEPH II

The documentary proof of the Emperor's contact with the philosophical movements of the eighteenth century, as well as of a consistent adherence to any particular system, has always been extremely vague. It may be for this reason that historians have conveniently classified him with Frederick II of Prussia and Catherine II of Russia as a disciple of the principles of the French Enlightenment. Whether Frederick and Catherine had any principles to speak of, except around the dinner table and in the pages of their writings, is still a debatable question.

Joseph undoubtedly did; but were his beliefs those of the Enlightenment?

" He read Voltaire who repelled him with his mockeries," wrote Pirenne, " and if he read Rousseau he did not understand him." [1] Voltelini, supporting the same point of view, maintained that the Emperor had no knowledge of Montesquieu or of the Encyclopedists.[2]

We know very little of Joseph's contacts with the leading spirits of the Enlightenment. Frederick II, after his famous meeting with the Emperor at Neisse, described the latter as a charming man who, "having had pedantic teachers, had enough sense to read Voltaire and to appreciate his merits." [3] On the other hand, Joseph, on returning to Austria from France, passed Voltaire's home at Lake Geneva without a visit. On being asked the reason for this omission, he remarked drily that he knew the Sage of Ferney "too well already." [4]

We know even less of Joseph's relations with Rousseau. The Emperor visited Jean Jacques during his stay at Paris. The conversation, we are told, was about music. Nevertheless, the fact that he visited the philosopher at all, especially in the last year of the latter's life, would somewhat temper Voltelini's statement that the Emperor regarded the author of the *Social Contract* as a dangerous man.[5]

Joseph was undoubtedly influenced by the guiding ideas of the French philosophers, and still more perhaps by their spirit. Their main demands, the abolition of serfdom, toleration, equality before the law, and the reduction of censorship were also his principal objectives. " Reason and humanity " was his motto as well as theirs.

1 Henri Pirenne, *Histoire de Belgique*, Brussels, 1921, V, 378.

2 Hans von Voltelini, " Die Naturrechtlichen Lehren und die Reformen des 18ten Jahrhunderts," *Historische Zeitschrift*, Munich, 1910, X, 67.

3 Saul K. Padover, *The Revolutionary Emperor*, London, 1934, p. 30.

4 *Ibid.*, p. 128.

5 H. von Voltelini, *op. cit.*, p. 67.

In the economic field he knew and esteemed Turgot, although Joseph himself has told us that when he entered the Council of State for the first time he did so as a staunch adherent of Colbert.[6] His repudiation of Colbert, nominally at least, followed very quickly,[7] and for a long time and by many, the Emperor was considered a follower of the *économistes*. This notion was given support by the physiocratic form which many of his utterances were to take: " The soil, which nature has given for the maintenance of mankind, is the sole source from which all comes and to which all flows back." [8] This was good orthodox doctrine indeed. But many of the provisions of his laws were completely contrary to physiocratic teachings. " It has often been said, at least in Germany," wrote Mirabeau, " that the Emperor wanted to introduce the physiocratic system into his states. Good Heavens! What kind of physiocracy is it when there are tolls and custom barriers, not only toward foreign countries, but from one province to another, when the people have neither liberty nor property rights?" [9] Mirabeau, in all matters concerning Joseph and Austria, was a highly unfriendly and prejudiced critic. But in this instance his criticism is probably just, or at least it would be if Jospeh had ever claimed to be a member of the physiocratic school. This, however, he did not do. " As far as economic Articles of Faith are concerned," he wrote at the age of twenty-four, " I am an atheist." [10] And atheist he remained for the rest of his life. He adopted the language of one doctrine, he borrowed the methodology of another, but the content was and remained essentially " Josephian."

6 A. von Arneth (ed.), "Denkschrift Kaiser Joseph II," *Maria Theresia und Joseph II, Ihr Briefwechsel*, Vienna, 1867, III, 337.

7 *Ibid.*, p. 337.

8 J. F. Bright, *Joseph II*, London, 1905, p. 145.

9 Honoré de Mirabeau, *De la Monarchie Prussienne*, 7 vols., London, 1788, VII, 378-9.

10 A. v. Arneth, "Denkschrift Kaiser Joseph II," *op. cit.*, p. 337.

What then were the real roots of the Josephian principles if the Emperor's contact with French philosophical thought was essentially too ephemeral, his acceptance of it too qualified for us to consider it the basic core of his philosophy?

The problem is indeed a difficult one. Mirabeau, pondering over the same question in the last years of the Emperor's life, burdened Hornick's *Oesterreich Ueber Alles Wann Es Nur Will* with the whole responsibility. "It contained," he wrote, " the whole economic system of the Emperor." [11] Mirabeau, like many of his contemporaries, may have exaggerated the importance of Hornick as an individual,[12] but his contention probably points in the right direction. The theories of the Austrian cameralists were probably much closer to the thought of the Emperor than Voltaire or Rousseau could ever have been.

From the point of view of closeness and frequency of contact alone this seems a defensible thesis. Justi had lectured at the Theresianum at Vienna during Joseph's youth. Martini, himself a student of Rieger,[13] had taught the young Archduke " Natural and International Law." Of the latter's close acquaintance with Joseph von Sonnenfels there can be no question.

Perhaps this balancing of native versus foreign influences presents a somewhat one-sided picture. After all, the intellectual roots of eighteenth-century cameralism and of the Enlightenment are found in the same soil, and of the influence of the *philosophes* on their German contemporaries there can be no doubt. Was not Justi himself, in attempting to refute Montesquieu, forced to approach the problems of society in much the same manner in which the latter had posed them? [14] Was not

11 H. de Mirabeau, *op. cit.*, VI, 268.

12 Albion Small, *The Cameralists*, Chicago, 1910, p. 130.

13 Paul Rieger was the first scholar to hold a chair for Natural Law at the University of Vienna.

14 Quoted in Luise Sommer, " Die Oesterreichischen Kameralisten," *Studien zur Sozial- Wirtschafts- und Verwaltungsgeschichte*, Vienna, 1920, p. 214.

his statement that " fortunately the personal interest of every human being always corresponds to the welfare of the community as a whole " [15] a surprisingly close parallel to the theories of economic individualism?

Yet Joseph's acceptance, as far as we can speak of acceptance, of the native rather than the foreign form of Enlightenment was, it would seem, more than an accident. The state, the economy, the institutions which Justi and Sonnenfels discussed in their writings were also the state, the economy, the institutions which Joseph knew in practice. The concrete background from which they drew their theories was also the land which Joseph had been called upon to govern. The doctrines which they advocated were therefore designed to solve his problems. In many cases he made this solution so much his own that in some instances, in Sonnenfels' case for example, it is never quite clear whether the philosopher was the inspiration of, or the apologist for, Joseph's actions.

We have already spoken of the similarity between the theories of the cameralists and the philosophical thought of Western Europe. There were, however, important distinctions, distinctions which, it may be presumed, are primarily due to the difference in historical development between the Western European countries and the Germanies.

Sonnenfels, in repudiating Rousseau, contended that not man alone but man in society constituted the natural state. Consequently to free man from bondage it was not absolutely essential to give him personal freedom, as the philosophers of the West had contended, but primarily necessary to deliver him from the special class and corporate loyalties to which he had so far been chained. In short, all groups intermediary between the individual and the state, the estates, the Church, the guilds, were to be deprived of their political importance. And, fortunately, again by dint of the pre-established harmony which existed between the

15 *Ibid.,* p. 239.

welfare of the individual and the state, the procedure would not only free the subjects but at the same time contribute to the consolidation of the state and enable the latter to present a united front against foreign countries. What we have here then is a theory of *étatisme,* not very different from the practice of Henry IV, of Richelieu, or of Colbert a century earlier, except that it was now provided with the underpinnings of a natural rights' philosophy. And somewhere within the framework of this doctrine of enlightened mercantilist *étatisme* we seem to find most of the elements of the complicated system of theories and actions which history has come to call the "Reforms of Joseph II." One cannot help feeling that the impractical idealism, of which the Emperor has been accused, is of a form highly modified by practical considerations.

Joseph knew, as the whole world knew, that the Holy Roman Empire was falling apart. He knew that the future of the House of Habsburg rested with its hereditary lands, lands which were held together only by their common allegiance to the crown. But Joseph, with his curiously unexalted, almost pedestrian views on kingship no longer believed that a common sovereign was enough to hold far-flung provinces together. He set out to create stronger ties: a common law, a common language, a uniform system of administration. To achieve this aim he had to humble the nobles, the clergy, the non-German elements, he had to lift to equal status the Protestants, the Jews, the peasants, the illegitimate. He sought to carry out these measures with unwavering logic, regardless of personal considerations, regardless of protest, regardless of opposition. Joseph was by no means as unaware of the opposition he was going to encounter as some of his biographers would have us believe. But he felt that he had no choice. He knew only too well the character of the men who were likely to succeed him, he knew that what he himself did not do would be left undone.

We would, however, miss the real Joseph if we were to ascribe all his actions to a cold, logical system by which he tried to save the Austrian state. Despite his references to "state welfare" and the "state as a body" it seems clear that what he meant was the welfare of the individuals within the state. He had, for instance, a deep and lasting sympathy with the peasants in their wretched condition, and there was urgency in his desire to help them. Perhaps in this sense he was a fanatic. But Joseph, who had seen so much, observed so much, suffered so much, can hardly be blamed for not practicing the wise moderation of a Frederick who cared so little for human life.

Perhaps the Emperor cannot be blamed either when, in his eagerness to secure what he conceived to be the rights of the many, he was impatient with the privileges of the few. Privilege to him was an artificial institution, incompatible with the laws of nature and justice. He spared no effort to destroy its manifestations. With that biting irony for which he was to become famous, he attacked the position of the nobles:

> How wonderful is the career of an aristocrat; the insignia of a chamberlain, a position in the government are ready for him. He will use them by never entering his office. After all, such a position is the least that the government owes to his beautiful name, his ancestors or his family. Even if he and his brothers are recognized fools, they cannot be absent from the privy councillor's table because once upon a time their family produced a single honest and sensible man. The court must be happy when, without the slightest merit, such a man allows it to hang the ribbon of St. Stephan's Cross around his neck. If he goes on vegetating for a while after that, he can even become a Knight of the Golden Fleece.[16]

Joseph had no intention of perpetuating this situation. He argued that a man's ability did not depend on his rank and that consequently there was no reason to treat rank itself as an inviolate institution. He wrote in the famous reform proposals, submitted to Maria Theresa at the beginning of the co-regency, that he would

16 Quoted in Ernst Benedikt, *Kaiser Joseph II*, Vienna, 1936, p. 119.

accord liberty of marriage without distinction, even to those marriages which are today considered *mésalliances*. I know of no law, divine or natural, which would oppose them. It is only the law of prejudice which would make us believe that I am worth more because my grandfather was already a count, and because I own a parchment signed by Charles the Fifth. At birth we inherit nothing from our parents but animal life. Thus king, count, burgher or peasant, there is not the slightest difference.[17]

The attacks on the rights of nobles were bound to undermine the Emperor's position as an absolute ruler, which after all involved a much greater degree of privilege than the whole status of nobility. But in Joseph's concept of kingship there was no thought of divine ordination, nor probably even of the patriarchical idea of service to the state which Frederick had expressed in classic form. To the Emperor his office was a profession in which one worked hard to be successful. " Madam," he is said to have replied to a Parisian lady who asked him about his sympathies in the American war of independence, "it is my job to be king." [18] Even more characteristic perhaps is the letter to his sister Christina, written on the occasion of the Papal visit to Vienna in 1782. " As far as the question of Church and State is concerned," wrote the Emperor, " our views are unchanged. Each of us earns the bread he eats. He defends the authority of the Church and I uphold the right of the state." [19]

If he himself " earned his bread " the Emperor demanded that his subjects do likewise. He demanded of his officials the same tireless hard work, the same self-sacrifice, the same breadth of vision that he himself demonstrated. But what was possible to this man who, as he himself said, was " neither father, nor husband, nor son," was not possible to ordinary

17 A. von Arneth, " Denkschrift Kaiser Joseph II," *op. cit.*, pp. 353-54.

18 S. K. Padover, *op. cit.*, p. 120.

19 J. F. Bright, *op. cit.*, p. 140.

human beings. Yet the members of the bureaucracy were the only real assistants he had in the execution of his reforms. They were neither thoroughly trained nor animated by great ideals, a fact which will hardly surprise us if we remember that social and political thinking was itself woefully lacking, outside the circles of professional scholars, in eighteenth-century Germany.

All this Joseph knew well. The lack of education was the first general condition he attacked in his reform proposals:

> I begin with education. It is much neglected here. All the parents want is to see their children adopt certain attitudes which are in conformity with their own. The good souls believe that they have obtained everything and have made a great man for the state if their son attends mass, confesses every fortnight, prays his rosary, and reads only what the limited mind of his father confessor allows him to read. Provided then that he does not lift up his eyes or blush in society, that he keeps one hand on his belt and the other on his waistcoat, that he knows how to bow gracefully or to ask politely: "what time is it?" or "how are you?," who would be bold enough not to say, "what a nice boy, how well educated!" Yes, I would reply, if our state were a monastery and our neighbors chaplains.[20]

There is much of Joseph in this passage: his anti-clericalism, his concern for usefulness to the state, his impatience of form without content. In this, as in almost all other matters, it seemed to him that the existing state of Austria was in conflict with good sense, in conflict with the precepts of humanity. "Our present situation," he wrote fifteen years before his accession, "demands every attention and prompt remedy."[21] The principles by which this remedy was to be achieved were as clear to him in 1765 as in 1780 or 1785: the centralization of the Austrian state and the promotion of comparative equality among its members. For the fulfillment of this aim,

20 A. von Arneth, "Denkschrift Kaiser Joseph II," *op. cit.*, p. 348.
21 *Ibid.*, p. 335.

the emancipation of the Austrian peasant was an absolute necessity.

THE AGRARIAN THOUGHT OF THE LATER EIGHTEENTH CENTURY CAMERALISTS

Even before the accession of Joseph II, the eighteenth-century cameralists, Justi and Sonnenfels in particular, had done much to arouse the sympathy of the general public for the downtrodden peasantry. In works which ranged from poetry and fiction to the most technical essays on the reclamation of ponds and wastelands, they had brought the plight of the rural inhabitant before the eyes of their readers. The most attractive piece of fiction in this category is perhaps Sonnenfels' weekly, *The Man Without Prejudice*. Using the "man from the moon" technique, Sonnenfels invented a noble savage, Capa-kaum, whom he introduced to the mores and folkways of Austrian society. In order to acquaint his pupil with the social and economic aspects of rural life, Sonnenfels decided to take him on an extended journey to the country. There Capa-kaum was to meet the "first, the most venerable of all estates with its ploughs, with its flocks, in its quiet huts and . . . in its purity." Only thus would Capa-kaum learn to understand the peasant, never in Vienna, "where our spoiled eyes see everything in an inverted fashion, where conditions are determined by selfishness, where the most independent of all estates is subjected to those who cannot do without it." [22]

Happy to have saved Capa-kaum from the corruption of urban life, Sonnenfels bade farewell to the city:

> Fare thee well, Vienna, city of polish without politeness, of respectability without morals, of noise without occupation, where they sleep through the day and gamble through the night, where men become women and women dolls, where

22 Joseph von Sonnenfels, "Der Mann ohne Vorurteil," *Gesammelte Schriften*, 10 vols., Vienna, 1783, II, 172.

marriage is without love, company without friendship, where the fool is often honored and poverty always a disgrace, fare thee well, greener pastures call me.[23]

Once they had arrived in the country, Sonnenfels pointed out the importance, as well as the insecurity, of rural life to his pupil:

> You see, my friend, the sweat and toil of the peasants, the ripening seeds. On them depends the hope of the proud city . . . A dry season which robs the grain of its nourishment, a cloud which pours destructive hail upon the field, an army of locusts, . . . a thousand other accidents can destroy this hope. But they, the thoughtless ones [the inhabitants of the city], feast.[24]

Eventually the author and Capa-kaum reached a picturesquely situated little village. Capa-kaum could hardly wait to knock at one of the doors and enjoy the famous rural hospitality of which he had read so much in Homer. But as the door opened he recoiled in horror and Sonnenfels had him exclaim:

> How have my expectations been deceived! How different is this from what I believed to find and for which I hurried! Look at this woman! Where is the cleanliness which, together with purity and simplicity, is considered the charm and attraction of the rural hostess? These rags, with which she is only half covered, are a mark of misery and awake horror. And these naked children crawling on the floor, it seems that the dirty straw in the corner is their bed.[25]

Meanwhile the master of the house returned from his work in the fields. As he had no food to offer to the travelers, the author and Capa-kaum invited him to dine with them at the local inn. After a good meal and some wine the peasant,

23 *Ibid.*, II, 172.
24 *Ibid.*, II, 172.
25 *Ibid.*, II, 175.

who had been too shy to speak at first, became a little more confident and related to Sonnenfels and the utterly astonished Capa-kaum the conditions of the peasantry: not only was he poor, he said, but so were all his neighbors, all peasants in the whole country. Poverty was the only thing they were never without and were always able to leave to their children after their death.

> My God, what misery it is to be a peasant! The summer is spent in sweat, the winter in need. Our acres will hardly yield their seed if we cannot fertilize them. But where shall we get fertilizer when we have difficulty keeping even two horses? Pastures for the cattle do not exist except for the meagre common fields. Alas, the poor animals cannot live by air and dust alone! If it is a bad year, misery appears unannounced. Even if Heaven blesses our seeds, It does not bless them for us. The tithe, the dues, the seeds, the repayment of loans, when I have paid all that there is hardly anything left . . . Believe me, gentlemen, if the Empress knew our situation she would be sorry for us![26]

After having treated this poor but loyal subject of Maria Theresa to the best meal of his life, Sonnenfels and Capa-kaum moved on to another village. There conditions were even worse. The peasants were overburdened with week work and cartage duty and were being treated cruelly by the rural officials. Sonnenfels, bemoaning the callousness of society towards " its most useful members," mused that without agricultural laborers none of the other classes in society would be able to exist. Therefore these classes, if for their own selfish interest only, ought to show the peasant more consideration.

Next Sonnenfels and Capa-kaum crossed the Semmering into Styria. On the way Sonnenfels fell ill, an illness which provided an occasion for the patient to point out that " in this, as in most other things, society seemed to be completely un-

26 *Ibid.*, II, 180-2.

aware of these poor members. In the cities doctors, hospitals, pharmacies are to be found in abundance—here none." [27]

Upon the publication of these travel reports, Sonnenfels seems to have been deluged with angry letters from his readers. "Truly my good author," wrote one,

> the idea of getting lost in the country was rather capricious, if not grotesque. Do you really want to make the peasants more sensitive to their misery by telling them: You are miserable? The good people must know that themselves. If, on the other hand, your aim was to inform us, it is somewhat like traveling to India to warn us of the temptations of the new world . . . One more thing, my dear sir, do you believe that the subject about which you declaimed so passionately in the fifteenth and sixteenth issue of your paper, is a popular one? An artist painting a sick man disfigured by running sores, would arouse all the more repulsion the more exactly he reproduced nature. How is your dear peasant served by our sterile sympathy?[28]

"My favorite author," wrote another, "but not on the subject of black bread, tattered peasant women, or of any of the things which you have made us read lately." [29] Most annoying to Sonnenfels was a letter directed to his publisher at Vienna: "For the good of those for whom he is so zealous," wrote the anonymous correspondent, "please ask your author to do a little violence to his obstinacy, or if he so wishes, his firmness. If our dogs threaten to run away, we order the hunters to draw their leashes more firmly." [30]

To this Sonnenfels replied angrily:

> In the midst of writing about the peasantry, about the miserable conditions in which public order leaves them, about their oppression by the subordinate despots, I receive the order

27 *Ibid.*, II, 206-7.
28 *Ibid.*, II, 221-2.
29 *Ibid.*, II, 222-23.
30 *Ibid.*, II, 226.

to be silent. In order to make this command more effective
one has used the pretext that the little unrest which the
peasantry showed here and there, was the consequence of
these pages. What miserable nonsense! The peasantry does
not read, but some of its oppressors have read these lines.
Their content must have struck home, for one has tried to
tear the brush from the hand of the painter.[31]

While *The Man Without Prejudice* was designed to arouse
sympathy for the downtrodden rural population, Sonnenfels'
economic writings discussed the means to its salvation.

To Sonnenfels, as to most economic thinkers in Austria
at the time, a very large rural population was prerequisite
to any reform program. He spent some time and calculation
in trying to find the right ratio between peasants and other
classes of society. Eventually he gave up this pursuit, but
concluded that as long as there was uncultivated arable land,
a lack of agricultural laborers existed. As it was a recognized
truth that "this useful class of citizens could never be too
numerous in any state," it was the duty of the government to
prevent the increase of those groups which tended to swell at
the expense of the peasantry. Among them Sonnenfels named
"luxury arts, and other occupations of little value such as the
sciences, the servant folk and the poor." [32] Next the state was
to put a halt to the "insolvency of the peasant owners" and
to deal with the circumstances which caused it, fires, wars,
rinderpests and the like.[33]

Sonnenfels insisted, however, that none of these specific
measures could be successful, unless the peasant were given
secure and hereditary possession of the land he tilled. Here
again he followed the lead of Justi who, in *Grundfeste zu der
Macht und Glueckseligkeit der Staaten* (*Foundations of the
Power and Happiness of States*) had insisted that the whole

31 *Ibid.*, II, 226.

32 Joseph von Sonnenfels, *Grundsätze der Polizey, Handlung und Finanzwissenschaft*, Munich, 1787, p. 180.

33 *Ibid.*, pp. 183-211.

problem of the prosperity of a state centered around the
ownership of land. Only if the soil was in the hands of those
who worked it, did it fulfill its real function. This principle
was being violated in two ways: by serfdom and by insecure
tenancy. As long as such conditions existed Justi saw no great
hope that agriculture would flourish:

> As long as the peasants do not have complete property
> rights, they lack the most noble motive, the most effective
> incentive to cultivate their land to the best of their ability,
> for they must always fear that they or their children will
> be evicted. This confiscation is always the privilege of the
> landowner as far as serfs are concerned, and often hap-
> pens even to ordinary tenants. Such customs and rights,
> especially serfdom, are also in themselves so unjust, and so
> contrary to the nature and the character of the state, that
> one can only be surprised that, in reasonable and enlightened
> times like our own, they can still exist. The liberty of the
> citizen and of all members of the state is the first important
> quality of all civil constitutions. States where one estate or
> one class of people is subjected to another, have as monstrous
> a constitution as those which existed in the most barbarian
> times. Moral and reasonable epoches, like our own, cannot
> allow such institutions to continue without ignominy.[34]

Sonnenfels, like Justi, blamed the insecurity of peasant
owners on the faulty constitution of the country and pointed
out that, where such evils existed, effective legislation was always difficult. Then, using an argument typical of his time, an
argument put forth by Joseph II over and over again, namely
that the good and the useful could never be in conflict, he
went on:

> If the noble landowners would only realize that such a con-
> stitution is at war with their own best interests, they would
> not oppose its abolition so fiercely. A right based on length

34 Johann Heinrich Gottlob von Justi, *Die Grundfeste zu der Macht und
Glueckseligkeit der Staaten*, Koenigsberg, 1760, p. 149 ff.

of ownership is, moreover, made very doubtful by the older and imprescriptible rights of humanity.[35]

Sonnenfels felt that the right of the nobility to demand privileges had disappeared when the function for which these exemptions had been granted, the defense of the country, was taken over by the state. If the privileges of the nobility were rooted not only in tradition, but in a contract with the monarch, it would be more difficult to abolish them. Even then he was certain that a contract " with one part of the nation, to the disadvantage of the other, must always be greatly opposed, attacked, and not infrequently abolished." [36]

In this spirit Sonnenfels opposed evictions, and advocated the commutation of feudal services into money dues. " Experience confirms," he wrote, " how little politic is the axiom that the peasant works hardest when he is most miserable." [37] The state ought to guarantee rightful possessions to the landowner as to all other property holders. " But it must draw firmly the limits of his demands and protect the subjects against any increase, for whatever reason or under whatever pretext it may be asked.[38]

To insure greater justice to the peasantry Sonnenfels, like Justi before him,[39] advocated a tax on land, based on a new survey, by which the soil was to be resurveyed, reassessed in accordance with its production, its area, its position, and a uniform percentage levied upon it: " The tax on land," he wrote, " is part of the pure income from land. Consequently, if the land tax is not to lose its value and to degenerate into an

35 J. von Sonnenfels, *Grundsätze der Polizey, Handlung und Finanzwissenschaft, op. cit.,* p. 187.

36 *Ibid.,* pp. 357-8.

37 *Ibid.,* p. 188.

38 *Ibid.,* p. 366.

39 J. H. G. von Justi, *Staatswirtschaft,* 2 vols., Leipzig, 1758, I, 321-99.

ambiguous genus of land and personal tax, the status of the owner must not make for any kind of inequality." [40]

The theoretical writings of men like Sonnenfels and Justi outlined the way for the reforms of Joseph II. When the program went into effect Justi had died, but Sonnenfels became one of Joseph's foremost advisers, the man who is reputed to have drawn up many of the laws dealing with the emancipation of the peasants. Better than anyone else, perhaps, he has expressed the principles which guided the agrarian reforms of Joseph II:

> Humanity and the public welfare demand that the fate of the peasant be a bearable one. May he also participate in the general prosperity, may he be protected from the unjust demands of selfish lords! That being whom fate has sentenced to draw furrows in the sweat of his brow, will only plough his acres according to the hopes and thoughts which cheer him on while he labors . . . Only *legislation* will truly encourage him. [41]

THE ABOLITION OF PERSONAL SERFDOM

The reign of Joseph II began with a most significant and dramatic piece of legislation—the abolition of personal serfdom wherever it still existed. It was originally thought that this institution persisted only in the Slavic provinces and in Hungary. The decree of November 1, 1781, abolishing serfdom in Bohemia, Moravia and Silesia, spoke of the German provinces as the model for the altered relationship between peasants and nobles: " We have taken into consideration," wrote the Emperor, " that the abolition of serfdom, and the introduction of a moderate subjection, instituted according to the example of our Austrian hereditary lands, will have the

40 J. von Sonnenfels, *Grundsätze der Polizey, Handlung, und Finanzwissenschaft, op. cit.*, pp. 389-90.

41 J. von Sonnenfels, *Politische Abhandlungen*, Vienna, 1777, p. 117. The third sentence of the quotation is cited by Sonnenfels from Fortbonnais' *Elemens de Commerce*, chapter III.

most useful influence on the betterment of industry and agriculture, and that reason and humanity alike require this
change." [42]

Gradually, however, it became clear that the conditions
which the Emperor regarded as constituting serfdom existed
in several of the German provinces as well as in Bohemia,
Moravia and Silesia. [43]

While the Bohemian decree was still in preparation, the
Emperor approached most of the other estates in the monarchy
on the matter. The response was much the same everywhere.
The estates usually denied that serfdom existed in their province, explaining that the absence of freedom of marriage, freedom of movement, and of the right of the peasant to learn
arts and crafts was conditioned by a peculiar local situation
and had to be retained for the benefit of the peasant just as
much as, or even more than, for that of the landlord. The Emperor remained unconvinced by these explanations.

The Publication of the Edict. The first major clash in the
German provinces occurred with the Estates of Styria. The
government sent a circular asking that the " honorable local
estates " state firmly and speedily whether or not serfdom
existed in Styria, and if so, how it was to be abolished. The
Estates answered that " in the inner constitution of this province the word 'servile' is neither customary nor known, but
in several parts of the country there exists a kind of hereditary
vassalage which, with minor differences, can be considered
to approximate serfdom." The Estates declared themselves
incompetent to inform the government about the origins of

42 Karl Grünberg, *Bauernbefreiung, op. cit.,* II, 390. Vol. II of *Bauernbefreiung* is a collection of sources.

43 F. von Hauer, *op. cit.,* I, 50 ff., quotes a law of November 1, 1781, for
Lower Austria, the text of which is identical with that of the law abolishing serfdom in Bohemia, Moravia and Silesia. With reference to him
A. Mell, *op. cit.,* p. 172 states that serfdom was abolished in Lower Austria
on November 1, 1781. I have not found any other reference supporting
this view.

that institution or to judge the efficacy of the Bohemian law.[44]

The Emperor was furious at their insolence and sent them a blistering letter charging them to elaborate on each point of the Bohemian law in detail. The body of that law consisted of six short and concise provisions: The serf was free to marry whom he wished, he might devote himself to arts and crafts as he desired, and, if he observed the provisions relating to conscription (*Werbbezirkssystem*) move from place to place, settle down or seek employment in any part of the monarchy. The consent of the landowner was to be merely formal and without cost to the ex-serf. The compulsory service of children at the court of the lord was also abolished, except in the case of orphans who had been brought up on the manor and whose obligations were limited to three years. The last provision of the law confirmed the continuation of the *urbarial* patents with regard to feudal services but stated categorically that, apart from these, "no burden can be imposed on the subjects. Least of all can anything be demanded from them under the pretext of their previous servitude, since they are now to be regarded as free human beings." [45]

Concerning freedom of marriage the Estates answered that it had formerly been restricted to put a halt to the procreation of the "idle charity-seeking rabble," but that this was no longer the case. Each subject could now marry without difficulty. On point two, freedom of movement, the Estates were adamant. They declared that the constitutional and documented freedom of the Estates of Styria allowed them to control their subjects' movements and to collect fees on departure. These rights had been repeatedly confirmed by Imperial resolutions. The provision dealing with the rights of peasant children to learn arts and crafts, the Estates thought unnecessary since that right had always existed in Styria. They admitted that "customary orphan services were demanded in

44 A. Mell, *op. cit.*, p. 175.

45 *Handbuch*, I, 74 ff.

several parts of Upper Styria," but did not specify what they meant by "customary." The last provision of the law they found redundant, because, as they pointed out, they were bound by the laws regarding labor services in any case. In summary they stated that the kind of situation which the government hoped to introduce into Bohemia already existed in Styria in all respects except freedom of movement, and that that privilege could not be granted to the peasants without breach of the constitutional rights of the Estates. Therefore the whole decree was inapplicable to Styria.[46]

The Emperor received the report of the Estates, footnoted by rather stringent criticism of it by the Chancellery. He seems to have had no doubt what the actual conditions were. His answer to the Chancellery was short and dry:

> As the word "serfdom," as the estates claim, is no longer known in the Inner Austrian lands, and as at present we are only dealing with some effects of serfdom that are either residues of former times or have crept in gradually, it seems that the word serfdom must be omitted from the patent. Concerning the content of the patent, it is necessary to establish without exception the personal freedom granted by the Bohemian and Moravian decree. This freedom, as is definitely known to me, does not at all exist in Lower Styria.[47]

The decree finally published for Styria was almost identical in content with the law for Bohemia, Moravia and Silesia, except that it said nothing about the abolition of serfdom. There seems to be a spark of mischievous humor in the action, but there was also deep anger. The preface, which replaced the idealistic preamble of the other decrees was harsh and cold: "Agriculture and industry," wrote the Emperor, "can only flourish under a decent freedom." The phrase about reason and humanity was conspicuously absent. The utilitarian

46 A. Mell, op. cit., pp. 176-8.
47 Ibid., p. 183.

motivation, the Emperor must have reasoned, was all the materialistic Styrians could understand.[48]

On July 12, 1782, a month and a day after the publication of the decree for Styria, serfdom was abolished in Carinthia. Apparently not much fuss was made. In the statute book the patent comprises two lines, which read: " In the Duchy of Carinthia, serfdom was abolished according to this regulation [the Bohemian decree]." [49]

The patent for Carniola also conformed to the Bohemian statute; but in that province, which probably was more rather than less feudal than Bohemia, the paragraph concerning freedom of movement had to be considerably modified. The peasant was forced to find a capable substitute before moving and to pay a fee on departure, while in other provinces this payment had been considered abolished by the grant of freedom of movement. " To prevent the oppression arising from this tax," however, the fee was legally limited to five per cent of his property.[50]

Effects of the Abolition of Serfdom. The effects of this abolition of serfdom remain to be considered. The most important consequences would naturally arise out of what was easily its most notable provision, the paragraph granting freedom of movement. This was the provision most stubbornly contested by the Estates of Styria, the provision which the government did not even introduce into Carniola in its full implications. While it affected only potentially those peasants who had bought or rented their land, it did have immediate implications for domestic servants. In several instances cooks, maids and coachmen are said to have packed up their belongings and to have left noble ladies to their own devices. Whether this was largely true or not is hard to ascertain, but the example was used by the nobles as an argu-

48 *Ibid.,* p. 184.

49 *Handbuch, op. cit.,* I, 77.

50 *Ibid.,* I, 77-9.

ment against freedom of movement. To counter these charges Joseph issued a number of servant regulations. Apparently the first of the series was the law for Lower Austria published on March 27, 1784. It is typical of the rest.

Its preamble stated that the " influence which the serving-folk have, not alone upon domestic peace, but also on the public order, has caused his Majesty to publish the present regulation for the rural population of Lower Austria."

The law obliged the servants to appear for their new position once they had taken earnest-money, to bring their own clothes, but exempted them from any responsibility for the tools they used. If they stole, the law obliged the master to bring the case to court. It even threatened him with three days on bread and water if, in a good-hearted mood, he failed to denounce thieves to the authorities. The master was also forbidden to lend out his own servants or to borrow those of another employer. Both employer and employee were to give six months' notice before terminating the period of service, " either from St. Jacob's to Candlemas or from Candlemas to St. Jacob's." After disposing of a peasant's legal exit from his master's house, the law turned to an elaborate discussion of illegal departures and prescribed strict penalties for fugitives. The last, and perhaps most interesting, provision of the statute prohibited agreements among servants for the purpose of forcing up wages. It forbade them to threaten to leave service simultaneously or to promise not to replace one another.[51] Collective bargaining clearly had not penetrated the mind of Joseph II.

The question of the fees on departure was in itself less important than the servant problem, but it clearly foreshadowed the attitude which the nobility was to take on the larger and more fundamental reforms which the Emperor was already preparing. Now, as in many later cases, they decided to ignore the Imperial verdict and cheerfully continued to demand what

51 *Ibid.*, VI, 24-45.

had been abolished once and for all. The question led to a protracted argument between the Imperial authorities and the nobles. The former explained that, since the subjects were now free men and had the right to move from place to place, they could no longer be forced to pay for that right, and the latter expressed their surprise at the existence of such a law. The Emperor first attempted to define the state of existing legislation by a law of August 1, 1783,[52] but eventually decided to wipe the whole slate clean:

> As a consequence of our concern for the liberty of our subjects, we have found it well that, after the abolition of serfdom in all provinces, freedom of movement should also be extended. The present law shall become effective in all Bohemian, Austrian and German lands, including Galicia, on the first of May. All previous laws regarding fees on departure are completely abolished.[53]

While the law abolished all taxes on departure within the German and Bohemian lands, those for migration to Hungary remained, but were limited to ten percent of the peasant's property. Finally a law of July 5, 1789, exempted the trousseau of persons marrying abroad and the vehicles of emigrants.

Another provision of the law abolishing serfdom, the right to marry according to one's choice, also met with serious difficulties. The Emperor had considered this a particularly important reform, partly because he had always insisted that the ability to choose one's life companion without impediment was the right of every human being, and partly because he felt that its institution would contribute to the growth of the population. In agreement with the cameralists, he considered such an increase indispensable to the state's welfare and security. To this end he had done everything to facilitate the marriage possibilities of the so-called "fallen women," the number of whom, to judge from the intense interest taken in

52 F. v. Hauer, *op. cit.*, I, 204-6.
53 *Handbuch, op. cit.*, IX, 399-404.

them both by cameral writers and by government legislation, must have been quite considerable. The " stain of dishonor " which their conduct had incurred was legally removed and " no obstacles whatever [were] to be put in the way of any person desiring to marry such a female." [54] The new code of criminal law abolished the concept of illegitimacy and removed all disabilities arising therefrom, while its clauses on pregnancy mitigated the lot of unmarried mothers.[55]

The leading personalities in the provinces, however, had their own views on the subject. Most sharply perhaps did the conservative Tyrolese disagree with the official point of view. By 1790 they had become so alarmed at the spread of poverty in their province that they reached the conclusion that poor people, far from being accorded " liberty of marriage without distinction," should be prevented from marrying at all.[56]

Domestic and Foreign Reaction. The decree abolishing serfdom had not in itself constituted an attack on the basic structure of the manorial system. Joseph himself saw clearly that, as long as labor services and patrimonial justice continued, there could be no complete liberation. But for the moment he thought that it was more important to establish the peasant as a personally free human being in society. Even this was distasteful to the nobles who, as a rule, were very contemptuous of their peasants. " The landowners," wrote Mitrofanov, " demanded not only work and money, but also subjection and awe." [57] And, whether by accident or because the nobles felt that they must now assert themselves and show that they were still the masters, this attitude became only intensified after the first Josephian reforms. As a countermeasure the Emperor forbade the peasant to kiss the hands of the master, or to bow to earth before him. Mitrofanov claims that the Emperor con-

54 *Ibid.,* VI, 113-14.

55 *Ibid.,* I, 163-4.

56 P. P. Mitrofanov, *Joseph II,* Vienna, 1910, p. 482.

57 *Ibid.,* p. 606.

sidered this a particularly important reform, "a visible sign that serfdom had been abolished." [58]

The opposition to the abolition of serfdom came not only from the nobles, but also from the representatives of the towns who apparently felt that the new position of the peasants would rob them of their importance in society.[59]

From abroad also, condemnation became vocal. "There is nothing more illusionary than this pretended liberty which does not do anything but exercise the pens of the newspaper writers and give Europe something to talk about," wrote Breteuil to Vergennes, "the lords and proprietors lost a great deal, without the peasant really gaining anything." [60]

Mirabeau too was so blinded by his hatred of Joseph II that he became untrue to his own principles and maintained that since "the peasants had become so brutish by their long servitude that they did not know what to do with their freedom," [61] serfdom should never have been abolished.

In other quarters, the measure was highly appreciated. In his first lecture of the academic year 1782, Sonnenfels paid a glowing tribute to recent social legislation and to the man who had been responsible for its introduction:

> He has given to the useful agricultural population, whose happy condition wise princes have always considered the glory of their governments, and which is recognized by all men as the strength of states, as that class of subjects which is the mother and provider of all others, the original rights of humanity, the membership in civil society which had been denied to it. From the memorable moment of this decision, may the word "servitude" no longer by spoken among us! All of Joseph's subjects are citizens.
>
> The despotism of oppressive princes over their peoples is an abomination. But the most abominable, the most un-

58 *Ibid.*, p. 606.

59 *Ibid.*, pp. 628-9.

60 *Ibid.*, p. 628.

61 H. de Mirabeau, *op. cit.*, VI, 499.

bearable despotism is that which citizens exercise over their fellow-countrymen. That was serfdom, that stain on any constitution wherein it is tolerated, the shame of the so-called sciences of law which argued human beings down to commodities, the disgrace of reason which thought up spurious grounds to defend oppression. Never has defenseless weakness given the stronger a right over it, except for the purpose of entrusting it with its own defense and best interest. Never has any confidence been more infamously violated than when the right of protection was turned into the right of the master, and creatures, which came from the hand of nature provided with the same strength of body and ability of spirit, were dragged down to be the property of their fellow creatures. How in the name of reason could men, even to protect their lives, have wished to sell that which constituted the greatest, the only value of life? How could a few thousand healthy, hard-working, vigorous creatures ever become the property of a weakling born of degenerate parents, or of a clever monk whose deputy today calls the father of the house for week work by impatiently knocking at the same door where only yesterday one of his order humbly begged for food?

But while philosophy fights such an absurd, revolting paradox with the superior power of victorious truth, while academies announce prizes for a plan detailing how sighing humanity can be freed from this yoke—*Joseph acts*.[62]

The Peasants and the Reforms in Administration and Justice

The sense of order, the desire for uniformity, which pervaded all the governmental reforms of Joseph II, was perhaps nowhere as evident as in his reforms in the fields of administration and justice. Here again he built on what Maria Theresa had begun. The *Kreisaemter* in civil administration, the limitations on patrimonial courts in the administration of justice, had been initially her reforms. But what was half-hearted and

62 J. von Sonnenfels, "Die Erste Vorlesung in dem Akademischen Jahrgang 1782," *Gesammelte Schriften, op. cit.*, VIII, 128-30.

vague under the Empress became systematic and methodical under Joseph. The Emperor aimed to separate justice from administration and civil from criminal justice.

Administration. The Estates had no place in such a scheme. Their meetings were limited to the occasions when it might please the Emperor to call them, and their standing committees were reduced to two members who, moreover, were to be attached to and approved by the provincial government. As the administrative functions of the Estates decreased, the local governments became more important. Like many a young bureaucracy they were growing too quickly to be well organized. Constant circulars on their duties were published and frequently they were asked to speed their labors. To achieve uniformity, the number of officials employed by the local administration was limited to the head of the *Kreisamt*, three to four commissioners, secretaries, clerks, apprentices, three dragoons, a physician, a surgeon, and a midwife. In his eagerness to see these officials fulfill the tasks he had outlined for them, the Emperor took a step for which he has been severely criticized ever since—the introduction of the lists of conduct. These lists, designed to check on the zeal and aptitude of the bureaucracy, have become infamous as a vicious weapon by which a tyrant spied on his officials. They asked for rank, name, age, years of service, marital status, number of children, special knowledge and aptitudes, religious conduct, attitude towards superiors and colleagues, and financial standing.[63]

In the beginning there was little opposition to this innovation. When the question was first discussed in the Council of State, its members objected only that superiors would be too soft-hearted to mention any but the pleasant qualities of their subordinates.[64] As it turned out, superiors were not always so kind. The Emperor, moreover, attempted to exercise personal control, at least over the higher officials. He caused quite

63 *Handbuch, op. cit.,* V, 119-20.

64 K. von Hock and H. I. Bidermann, *Der Oesterreichische Staatsrath,* Vienna, 1879, p. 133.

a sensation when he insisted that Count Christian von Thuer-
heim, Governor of Austria above the Enns, be sentenced to a
considerable money fine for failing to take a real interest in
the complaints of certain peasants against their lord.[65]

That Joseph II was by no means happy about the state of
his officialdom is easily seen from the famous "pastoral
letter," addressed to the members of the bureaucracy in the
year 1783:

> Three years have passed since I was forced to take over the
> administration of the state. I have during that period made
> known my priniciples, thoughts and intentions, with great
> difficulty, care and patience.
>
> I have not stopped at ordering a matter once, I have
> worked it out and explained it. I have corrected conditions
> arising from deep-seated prejudices, and have fought old
> customs by enlightenment . . . I have sought to instill
> into every official the love I feel for the general welfare and
> my zeal for its service. I have given confidence to the heads
> of departments, in order that they may influence the thoughts
> and actions of their subordinates . . . I therefore find it
> part of my duty, and of the complete loyalty which I have
> given to the state all my life, to insist with the utmost ser-
> iousness upon the fulfillment of the orders and principles
> which, to my utmost regret, I have seen very much neglected.
> I see that a great deal is ordered, but that little attention is
> paid to execution. Orders must be given repeatedly since most
> matters are treated without real interest. In this mechanical,
> servile manner, it is impossible to carry on public administra-
> tration . . . In all offices every single person must work
> with such zeal that he does not count hours, or days, or pages,
> but strains every nerve to the utmost in order to serve com-
> pletely according to expectation and according to his duty.
>
> Since the good can only be of one kind, namely that which
> serves all, or at least the greatest number . . . and since
> equally all provinces in the monarchy must constitute only
> one whole, all jealousy, all prejudice, which until now has

existed frequently among nations must cease . . . Nation,
religion, must not make the slightest difference, and as
brothers in a monarchy all must strive to be useful to one
another.

He who wishes to serve the state must think of himself
last . . . Only one intention can guide his action, the greatest good and usefulness for the greatest number.[66]

In order that the local government be able to fulfill these
stern principles, its heads were instructed to take yearly journeys through the provinces. On these travels they were to act
as the eyes and ears of the government at Vienna and to pay
particular attention to " the general condition of the population as well as the state of agriculture, industry and commerce." [67]

In his general solicitude for the underprivileged the Emperor
also asked the department heads to pay " exact attention how
the property of minors and insane was administered." [68] He
demanded, moreover, that the nobles send annual reports
about their conduct of the financial affairs of orphans to the
provincial government.[69]

While such important functions were being allocated to the
provincial and local governments, the main complaint of the
centralists during the time of Maria Theresa remained: the
Imperial officialdom in the provinces still consisted mainly of
members of the old feudal nobility.

After an inspection tour of the Inner Austrian provinces
in the year 1784, Joseph II wrote to the Governor, Count
Khevenhueller: " The ancestral pride of this province may
well be satisfied. Proportionately a great many more nobles
with ' sixteen ancestors ' than knights or scholars are employed

66 *Handbuch, op. cit.*, V, 181-201.
67 *Ibid.*, IX, 873-4.
68 *Ibid.*, IX, 873.
69 *Ibid.*, XVI, 929.

by the provincial government. *Opto ut prosit.*[70] Believing that the " sixteen ancestor " mentality was particularly dangerous to his program of reform, Joseph asked that the count and his subordinate officials pay more attention to the Imperial circulars and orders. He concluded with the following passage which again shows those twin traits of the Josephian reform spirit, a profound awareness of the difficulties in the way, and yet a hope and grim determination to surmount them:

> All beginning is difficult, especially when human beings are awakened and torn from their prejudices, from the slow pace which has become their second nature, and from the routine in which they have slept calmly, easily and blissfully and which has brought them honors, titles, status, and financial compensation as well.[71]

The Emperor thought, however, that " with never-ending patience, constancy and earnestness," the bureaucracy could be educated to act in a new spirit of thoughtfulness and efficiency. Once this spirit had become second nature, the officialdom would form an instrument by which the arm of the government at Vienna could reach into the remotest corners of the country. By two major methods, which as a working principle were only one, the elimination of the administrative functions of the nobility and the creation of an efficient bureaucracy, the peasant was to be brought into direct contact with the central government.

Justice. In the administration of justice, the same centralizing spirit made itself felt. A hierarchical system of authority, running parallel to the gradation of village community, district and provincial government in civil administration, was established.

The patrimonial tribunals remained courts of the first instance for the peasants, but their functions were rigidly cir-

70 Adam Wolf (ed.), " Ein Handbillet Kaiser Joseph II," *Beitrage zur Kunde Steiermärkischer Geschichtsquellen*, Gratz, 1875, XII, 156.

71 *Ibid.*, p. 156.

cumscribed. The most important pieces of legislation in this respect were the Law Concerning Subjects (*Untertanspatent*) and the Penal Law (*Strafpatent*), both published on September 1, 1781.

The Law Concerning Subjects, in a long and rather complicated exposition, explained the procedure by which a peasant could bring complaints against his lord. If the subject brought these claims before the patrimonial judge with befitting modesty, the lord was to answer such complaints within a limited period of time. If the claim developed into a legal action, the case was to be appealed to a further court. In such instances the government provided the peasant with the services of the so-called subject's advocate (*Untertansadvocat*), a government lawyer, who was to represent the peasant free of charge.[72] Joseph II did not initiate the idea of appointing such an attorney. It originated during the time of Maria Theresa, when one lawyer in each province was designated to represent the subjects in court action. But, as a result of the agrarian legislation of Joseph II, the functions of this office became of wider importance and were more rigidly defined:

> The advocate shall help subjects, asking for advice with becoming modesty, by counsel and deed. He shall inform them about their affairs according to his own best knowledge and conscience. He is to behave with correctness and punctuality and to follow the directions of the Law Concerning Subjects. He is to represent the rights of the subjects faithfully and to the best of his ability. He shall give them all necessary support.[73]

The advocate was authorized to take the case of the peasant through various judicial instances and as a last recourse even to " His Majesty personally." For this purpose another official, the subject court agent (*Untertanshofagent*), had been

72 *Handbuch, op. cit.*, I, 27 ff.

73 F. von Hauer, *op. cit.*, II, 102-3. From the instruction to the *Kreisamt* accompanying the Patent of September 1, 1781.

established in Vienna. It was one of the first acts of the government of Joseph II to decree that only through this officer could complaints reach the Emperor. The same law stated that the agent's name was Joseph Anton Wells and that his residence was on the third floor of a house called *Todtenkopf* (skull) in the Bognerstrasse.[74]

While the assistance of the government lawyer to the peasants was free of charge, the nobles indirectly had to pay part of his fee if they lost the case. The law of December 1, 1785, declared that " if the lords, in court action against their subjects, are adjudged the reimbursement of the expenses, the sum goes in part to the fiscal office (advocate's fee) and the rest to the subjects." [75] The nobles, perhaps not without reason, felt that here was social justice with a vengeance, for the law not only made the peasant's right to sue his lord incontrovertibly clear, it made such action of no cost whatever to the former, while the latter had to bear his own expenses, even if the complaints against him proved unjustified. The state had definitely declared itself the protector of the peasants.

At the same time as the Law Concerning Subjects, the new Penal Law was also published. It was promulgated *jure regio,* without even so much as a consultation with the Estates. In effect it did away with the slight discretionary powers which were still left to the manorial courts, abolished money fines entirely and made prison sentences of more than eight days subject to the approval of the local government.[76]

In its administrative as well as procedural aspects, the Emperor attacked the traditional system of patrimonial justice. He decreed that landowners should in the future employ competent judges who had completed prescribed university studies and had passed an examination, usually with the Court of Appeals. If nobles wished to exercise the judicial functions

74 Patent of April 7, 1781, *Handbuch, op. cit.,* I, 17-18.

75 *Ibid.,* VIII, 12.

76 *Ibid.,* I, 48 ff.

personally, they themselves were to take the tests. Since as a rule they deemed it below their dignity to take examinations, there was a tendency to hire fairly well-educated men. It is perhaps not without interest to note that the new judges were compensated in money wages, while hitherto the guardians of justice had depended on fines and taxes in kind, like " cheese, sausages and pickled tongues." [77] for their livelihood. Not only the new judges, but present incumbents as well, were to be tested for their fitness for the posts they held by an examination given by the Court of Appeals. The Emperor desired that only those who were found worthy of their office should be retained and that " no others [should] be tolerated." [78] It is the general consensus of opinion that the administration of justice improved greatly. Even Mirabeau, the irreconcilable, admitted, although with some qualifications, that the result of the reform was satisfactory: " One has discovered clearly," he wrote, " that the reform produced, even in this imperfect state, many useful results which will greatly expedite and improve the administration of justice." [79]

Of course, there was also protest. Its leaders, as usual, were the Estates of Tyrol who thought that learning was a virtue highly unnecessary to a jurist. " In our poor country," they wrote, " things are very simple. Scholars, on the other hand, do not wish to bother about such bagatelles, for which they, moreover, lack the necessary adroitness and ability." [80] Needless to say, the Emperor was not impressed.

The reorganization of criminal justice did not follow until 1787. The number of criminal courts was drastically reduced, usually to one each district. The Emperor wanted to entrust the administration of justice only to courts which, " provided with a sufficient number of certified and

77 P. P. Mitrofanov, *op. cit.*, p. 550.

78 *Handbuch, op. cit.*, XIII, 434.

79 H. de Mirabeau, *op. cit.*, VII, 239.

80 P. P. Mitrofanov, *op. cit.*, p. 554.

well-paid men, deserve the confidence of the government and of the people, and are capable of carrying out their duty without private business and intentions." [81] The complete execution of this law was prevented by the death of the Emperor only two and a half years later. Its main significance lay in the fact that, apparently for the first time in the history of the Austrian state, it established equality before the law, regardless of rank.[82]

With the most influential groups in Austrian society, this idea was not very popular. Karoline Pichler thought "very unfair" the "stern justice which, levelling all before the law, condemned a count, a privy councillor, a respected gentleman . . . as if he were a laborer or servingman." [83] Yet this stern justice did bear fruit. Speaking of the judicial reforms of Joseph II, fifteen years after the Emperor's death, Georg Hassels, one of the well-known publicists of the time, wrote that the Emperor had "dug chicanery a grave." [84]

PEASANT LAND TO THE PEASANTRY

Joseph II was too much of a materialist, too firmly convinced of the importance of economic affairs in the lives of men, to believe that social and political reforms, like the abolition of personal serfdom, or the changes in the system of justice and administration, important as he held them to be, could in themselves establish the peasant as a free individual in society. Paralleling his social reforms we detect a great many schemes and plans to improve the economic status of the peasant. This effort was to find its culmination, and in a sense its destruction, in the *Urbarial* Patent of 1789. Even earlier

81 *Handbuch, op. cit.*, XIV, 905-16.

82 Alfons Huber, *Oesterreichische Reichsgeschichte*, Vienna, 1901, p. 273.

83 Karoline Pichler, *Denkwürdigkeiten aus Meinem Leben*, 2 vols., Munich, 1914, I, 118-19.

84 Georg Hassels, *Statistischer Abriss des Kaiserthums Oesterreich*, Nuremberg, 1807, p. 242.

the Emperor attempted innovations in the field of land ownership and inheritance.

Land Ownership. As Justi and Sonnenfels had advocated,
and as was generally consistent with his activities in other fields
of agrarian legislation, the Emperor attempted to secure to
the peasant hereditary possession of the land. But the
matter, as Joseph himself realized, was no black and white
proposition. The distinction between those peasants who had
bought their land and those who had not, immense though
it might seem in theory, was often very small in practice. The
advantage of ownership was primarily derived from the fact
that the peasant and his heirs could not be deprived of their
farm except in some very extreme cases. Actually protective
legislation and the lord's own interest made evictions fairly
rare in any event. On the other hand, those peasant's who had
not " bought themselves in " (*eingekauft*) could as a rule count
on more personal interest and greater protection from their
manorial lord. Many peasants of course could not really afford
to buy their lands and since in the past the purchase had often
been forced on them by nobles in financial distress (cases are
known where the land holder had been made to buy the land
two or three times), it was the task of the state not only
to facilitate the peasant's purchase of his farm, but at the same
time to protect him against being forced to do so by the overlord.

The law of November 1, 1781, emphasized both aspects of
the problem. " We hereby graciously provide," wrote the
Emperor, " that wherever the peasants do not yet hold property rights and make a request to obtain such rights, the
landowners shall accede for a small remuneration to the demand; . . . but," he continued

> since there is no doubt that the subject, mindful of the ad-
> vantage connected with ownership, will request it voluntarily,
> we forbid landowners to force peasants to purchase property
> against their will. The local administration will have to pay
> close attention to make sure that there is neither the slightest

compulsion, nor the subjection of peasants to burdensome conditions.

The law also provided that those subjects who already owned their lands should be able to " use, pawn, mortgage, sell or exchange " as they pleased, with the sole exception that lands attached to the farmhouse could not be sold without it. The peasant owner was also given the right to go into debt without the permission of the overlord, but the limit of his liability was set at two-thirds of the value of his property.[85]

The nobility reacted to this decree as it had reacted to most others—with suspicion. It was offended by the suggestion that its business dealings needed close supervision and angry at the 'serious curtailment of its rights to interfere with peasant affairs. As was to be expected, the hereditary acquisition of land by the peasantry progressed slowly. But, as in the time of Maria Theresa, the government could take little direct action short of forcing the owners to sell part of their land. The possibility was actually discussed in the Chancellery. It was, however, too revolutionary, even for the government of Joseph II, and was eventually rejected. Occasionally, as in a resolution of May 27, 1786, the conversion of leaseholds into freeholds was recommended, but little seems to have come of these recommendations.[86]

The Emperor, however, attempted to achieve his aim indirectly by making eviction almost impossible. The peasant could be driven from his land for only two reasons. One, as stated in the Law Concerning Subjects of 1781, was " as a last and most severe punishment." The Emperor warned the lords not to take such a step lightly, to consider the age and general health of the subject as well as any extenuating circumstances, and to apply this " ignominious and severe penalty only when milder punishments have remained without ef-

85 *Handbuch, op. cit.*, I, 79 ff.

86 *Ibid.*, X, 99.

fect." [87] In no case were the lords allowed to act without permission from the local government. At the same time the Emperor sent an instruction to the latter warning them that:

> The eviction of a peasant from his farm is a very hard punishment and one of last resort. It is therefore not to be inflicted lightly. The local administration is earnestly reminded and enjoined not to permit the lords to evict their subjects except for very important reasons as a last and extreme punishment.[88]

The second reason for which a peasant could be evicted was the accumulation of debts beyond the two-thirds mark set by the decree of November 1, 1781. Again such action was to be preceded by a most thorough investigation. The property of the subject was to be investigated " by two non-resident and therefore more impartial, sensible officials " in the presence of the peasant. The investigators were to draw up an inventory of the assets and debts of the peasant and to send it to the local government together with the lord's petition for eviction. The local administration then called the contending parties before it and, on the basis of the report, gave or refused its permission, leaving both parties free to take the case to court.[89] As these inquiries worked out in practice, the summoning of officials from another locality, while it increased the impartiality of the investigators, became a little too cumbersome and expensive. Two years later the government decided that "it is not always necessary to call in two non-resident officials to give the estimate, but sufficient if, *ex officio*, two honest and impartial judges from a neighboring village are present." [90] This, it thought, would lower expenses considerably.

87 F. v. Hauer, *op. cit.*, I, 355.

88 *Ibid.*, I, 353.

89 *Handbuch, op. cit.*, VIII, 7-8 (Law of April 18, 1785).

90 F. v. Hauer, *op. cit.*, I, 358.

As the peasant could no longer be evicted, except in rare cases, he could not be forced to sell his land, even if he held it in usufruct only. Even if the lord found a peasant who was willing to buy the holding,[91] he could not evict the present tenant. The lords were also prohibited from exchanging some of their own land for peasant holdings or from confiscating fields as a means of exacting unpaid dues or taxes. All land which had been taken from the peasants for that purpose since the year 1776 was to be returned. If that was impossible, the lords were to "compensate the peasants in kind or equivalent."[92]

Inheritance Rights. The ideal vision of Austrian agrarian thought in the eighteenth century was a land of small peasant owners, living on prosperous farms in the possession of legal hereditary rights. Short of achieving this ideal it aimed to secure for the peasant at least the hereditary use of the land he inhabited. It is in this light that we must view most of the measures taken by the government of Joseph II with regard to peasant inheritance. The problem, as we have seen in the previous chapter, revolved largely around the question of free divisibility. The discussions on the subject in the Council of State are said to have been heated. Both Kees and Froidevaux advocated divisibility. The rest of the members, however, were in favor of the existing custom of entail (*Bestiftungs-zwang*). The Emperor also was opposed to free divisibility, mainly because he feared that its consequence would be detrimental to the continued growth of the population:

> The main problem for the state is whether a peasant holding shall be possessed by a single person, or dismembered and owned by several. Strong peasant holdings, occupied by large families, are much more useful to the state than smaller possessions. It seems, therefore, much more appropriate to declare the lands attached to the house as nonsalable and

91 *Handbuch, op. cit.,* VIII, 22-3 (Law of January 5, 1785).
92 *Ibid.,* XIII, 103-4.

inseparable, and allow only one son, be it the elder or the younger, to possess them, . . . but to regard the unattached lands as salable ... The peasant would be able to mortgage his farm, but in case of bankruptcy the creditor will have to take over the whole economic unit. He shall never be able to dismember it." [93]

The law of April 3, 1787, confirmed these principles. It designated the eldest son as legal heir, thereby preventing division of the farm unit through inheritance, as well as drastically limiting the nobles' right to choose among heirs. The overlords were given the privilege of raising objections against the heir, but in such cases the final decision rested with the local government.[94]

It had been customary in Austrian peasant usage to appoint the youngest son as heir, leaving to the stepfather the management of the farm until the heir became of age. Of this the law made a clean sweep. If the peasant's will did not appoint a guardian, the lord was authorized to do so, except that he could not choose the orphan's stepfather. In order that the child's inheritance should not be squandered before he reached maturity, all lands belonging to the holding were declared as " inseparable and indivisible." [95]

The major reason why the Emperor did not wish to see the stepfather administer the estate of a minor, was his opposition to the ownership of more than one holding by the same person. This principle when carried into effect aroused much opposition and eventually had to be repealed for the province of Tyrol.[96]

Joseph believed that small and medium-sized peasant holdings should be sold, bought, and inherited as a unit. On the other hand, he was very much in favor of the division of very

93 Johann Wendrinsky, *Kaiser Joseph II*, Vienna, 1880, pp. 231-2.
94 *Ibid.*, pp. 231-2.
95 *Handbuch, op. cit.*, XIII, 98-101.
96 Otto, Archduke of Austria, *op. cit.*, p. 39.

large peasant farms and even allowed a subsidy of fifty *Gulden* for each farm resulting from such a division, if it was not below forty *Metzen* (about 19 acres) of land.[97]

Pre-emption and Reversionary Right. Another condition which hindered the peasant's complete possession of the land he inhabited, even if he had actually bought it, was the persistence of two old feudal rights, the rights of pre-emption and of reversion. The right of pre-emption was first abolished on all lands owned by the clergy, then for all land of rustic, but not of domestic classification, and finally by a decree of March, 1787, almost completely.[98]

Reversionary right was abolished by a similar process. The law in this instance provided that if a contractual basis for this right existed it was to continue, but that no new contracts were to be drawn up. This prohibition, it was hoped, would in the course of time eliminate reversions altogether.[99] For some parts of Inner Austria the Emperor found that the gradual process would be too slow: " The detrimental consequences," read the decree for Inner Austria of March 31, 1788, " which arise for agriculture, and even for the morality of the peasant, from the existence of reversionary rights in Carinthia, have led to His Majesty's abolishing these rights altogether." [100] With the almost complete abolition of reversionary rights and of pre-emption, two other links in the chains which tied the peasant to his overlord were broken.

One cannot, in contemplating the agrarian reforms of Joseph II, help being amazed at how deliberately, methodically, and logically the Emperor went about his work. One is struck also by the complexity of the picture and the interdependence of its various aspects. It might not mean very much that the nobles could no longer determine peasant succession; but if

97 *Handbuch, op. cit.,* VIII, 17.

98 *Ibid.,* I, 105 and XIII, 144.

99 *Ibid.,* XVI, 908 (Law of October 22, 1788).

100 *Ibid.,* XV, 122-4.

one considers that the heir could sell or mortgage his property, or even leave the land altogether, that he need no longer
let the lord decide how his sons were to be educated, whom
they married, which of them went into the army, that the
threat of arbitrary punishment, which had always hung over
his head, was almost wholly eliminated, the result of the reform as it stood in the early fall of 1789 seems indeed impres-
sive. But the work was by no means completed. The most
fundamental attack on the manorial system, the measure to
which, as some historians have held, all previous innovations
were merely a prelude, the law which was to be the crowning
glory of the Emperor's agrarian legislation, was yet to come.

THE "PHYSIOCRATIC *Urbarium*"

In the beginning of 1789, the traditional institution of hereditary subjection (*Erbuntertänigkeit*) in Austria was deeply
shaken both morally and actually, but it still existed. It existed,
and would continue to exist, as long as its most salient feature,
the labor obligations of the peasant, continued to exist. For
their persistence the Emperor can hardly be blamed. He understood very well that, as long as part of the time and the
work of the peasant belonged to the overlord, the former
would never be free. But even Joseph did not dare simply
to abolish the claims of the nobles by royal fiat. Neither
could the state have compensated the owners, since the
Emperor had difficulty in balancing his budget even without
such an additional burden. In the beginning of his reign
Joseph had hoped that if he himself set a good example, the
nobles might follow. He had extended "Raab's System,"
which had been a great success under Maria Theresa, to many
royal and secularized estates. Again from all appearances
the scheme worked well. The Emperor even thought that it
worked so well that state subsidies for the commutation of
dues and services on private estates would be quite unnecessary: "The increased and certain income of domains that

have such an arrangement, the prosperous condition of the cameral and Jesuit subjects, and finally the mutual contentment and welfare are, and must be, the only attraction which will give rise to imitation by private estates." [101] " The abolition of labor services," wrote the Emperor in another connection, " is advantageous for the state, the lords and the subjects, if it is built on just principles." [102]

By a decree of February 10, 1783, he made clear what he thought these just principles were: labor services were to be commuted, at least for the greatest part; individual holdings on the lord's domain were to be distributed among the peasants who were also to be granted complete ownership of the "houses and acres already possessed by them in fact." The terms of commutation were given as one *Gulden* thirty *Kreutzer* for the thirteen days of labor services ordinarily discharged by an *Inmann,* and as five *Gulden* for a cottager's twenty-six day duty. A peasant who owed personal services only was to pay *three Gulden* for his house and two *Gulden* for each *Metzen* (about one half acre) of rustic land, and a subject who ordinarily fulfilled his obligations with teams, six *Gulden* for the house and eleven *Gulden* for each *Metzen* of land. The law re-emphasized that these fees had become a substitute, not only for week work in particular, but for all fees and services in general. It recognized the overlordship of the landowner, quoted the terms under which a peasant could be evicted,[103] and concluded that, except for such cases, no one could be deprived of his property and of the right of ownership connected with it.[104] A year later commutation contracts in some

101 *Ibid.,* I, 61-2.

102 P. P. Mitrofanov, *op. cit.,* p. 615.

103 The terms were identical with those discussed in the laws of September 1, 1781 and April 18, 1785, see pp. 124 and 125 above. Up to this point the decree consists mainly of quotations from the Patent of March 1, 1777.

104 *Handbuch, op. cit.,* I, 66-71.

regions could be drawn up free of charge.[105] The nobles paid
little attention to these provisions; it was the peasantry as
a labor force that was important to them, not the pecuniary
equivalent of the labor.

The Emperor was nonetheless determined to end labor services in some way. His effort met with universal disapproval.
Even the Chancellery, docile as a rule, opposed him on almost
every point. In the first debate on the subject only Friedrich
Eger, an ardent Josephian, agreed with the Emperor, and
the number of his supporters did not increase greatly at later
meetings. But Joseph would not give in; the *robot* had to go.

The services were not the only remaining injustice. The
peasants were still virtually the sole taxpayers, with a contribution that was out of proportion to their income as the
landowners' was small in relation to theirs. The Emperor had
always maintained that the question of taxation and that of
the services were one and the same. He therefore decided that
the solution to both problems was to be brought about by a
single master-stroke of economic legislation.

The plan itself was simple enough. It had been advocated
by both Justi and Sonnenfels, and had been in the air for
a long time. It provided that the existing distinctions which
divided land into noble, crown, peasant and Church lands
were to be wiped out. Then the land was to be resurveyed and
reassessed and a uniform percentage of its value levied upon it.
A part of this percentage was to go to the nobles as compensation for the loss of dues and the rest was to be paid to the
government in taxes.

But if the plan was simple, its execution was admittedly
difficult. The government had no staff that was either large
enough or well-trained enough to carry out so tremendous
a task; therefore the survey had to be executed within the
manorial organization. In a resolution of February 23, 1785,
the Emperor announced the new *cadastre* and asked all those

105 *Ibid.*, VI, 19 (Order for Graz, August 14, 1784).

who were to take part in it to acquire the tools necessary for
the purpose. Specifically, a manorial official in charge of the
" Book of Survey," was to be provided with a table and writing materials, two men were to carry and insert " six to
eight bars," and two others were to " draw the measuring
line." Finally " two rather grown up boys " were to " carry
the ten necessary nails in a little sack or purse." [106]

This resolution of January 23, was followed by a decree of
April 15, 1785. It announced the formation of a court commission in " domain and *robot* abolition affairs " under the
chairmanship of the " Privy Councillor and Court Vice-
chancellor, *Freiherr* von Gebler." The latter, a well-known
writer, author of *Der Minister,* was, like the hero of that play,
the prototype of the enlightened statesman of the period. Unfortunately he died before the survey got well under way.
Directly under the commission headed by Gebler, there was
to be a group of commissions, one for each province. Finally,
in each district the government appointed a subcommission,
consisting of a local government official and a steward from the
cameral estates.[107]

Once these prerequisites had been created, the whole plan
was outlined in a patent of April 20, 1785. In a preamble,
which is a typical product of mercantilist thought, as well
as of the Josephian pen, the Emperor announced that

> the existing tax system does not follow the precepts of equality
> and justice, neither among the German hereditary lands them-
> selves, nor among individual landowners. In addition, the
> principles upon which it rests are uncertain and detrimental
> to industry. Therefore His Majesty, as father and adminis-
> trator of the lands entrusted to him by Providence, has
> thought to lay the foundations for a new system of taxation
> by which, without increase in the present contribution, . . .
> each province, each community, each individual shall give

106 *Ibid.,* VIII, 54-6.
107 *Ibid.,* VIII, 60.

according to the fertility of the land, and therefore industry be liberated from all burden.[108]

To this purpose all arable land was to be surveyed and its probable produce estimated on the basis of past yields. The estimate was to be given by local landowners but the sub-commission was warned to examine such testimony closely.

Paragraph five of the law contained the usual appeal for speedy execution, couched in terms of economic motivation again typical of Joseph's legislation:

> The happy effect, which must be the consequence of a just system of taxation, is too important for His Majesty to permit any useless delay or tardiness. His Majesty therefore commands all landowners and judges, charged with carrying out the survey, . . . to work with extreme speed, in order that the *cadastre* can be drawn up this summer and autumn and be completed by the end of October.

Hoping to obtain the utmost cooperation from the landowners, the Emperor even compromised with circumventions of previous laws. He remitted in advance all penalties for those who had concealed part of their property in earlier surveys and ordered that no landowner be questioned if lands " which had hitherto been undiscovered . . . suddenly appeared." In conclusion he expressed the hope that " everybody will devote himself to this salutary regulation, the only intention of which is the general welfare, with patriotic, sympathetic zeal, and know how to beware of the disadvantage which disobedience will inexorably bring with it." [109]

The appendix of this law of April 20, 1785, instructed the surveyors regarding the classification of various types of arable land. In reading its provisions one becomes acutely aware of the difficulties of a land reform of this nature. How, for instance, was one to evaluate a pond, a waste or a garden

108 *Ibid.*, VIII, 61.
109 *Ibid.*, VIII, 62-8.

in comparison with fields and acres? The law divided the land into the following categories: arable land, wastes, ponds, meadows, gardens, pastures, bushes, vineyards, woods. Different methods of calculation were to be applied to the various categories. The produce of the acres was to be arrived at by taking the average of its grain yields for the nine-year period from 1774 through 1782. The ponds presented a special problem. It was eventually decided that they were to be registered at the value " of the neighboring acres comparable to them in fertility, because . . . most of them can be drained and cultivated, while fisheries in ponds must be regarded as industries." The produce of the meadows was to be measured by the bails of hay harvested from them. Gardens and pastures were to be treated in the same fashion. Woods were to be " measured by the owners themselves by the cord and the difference between hard and soft wood." [110]

In order that the peasants engaged in this work would be able to devote themselves to it with the necessary zeal, they were freed from all personal labor duty and from half the services performed with teams.[111] Like most tax reforms, the project was accompanied by the rumor that the government was secretly aiming at a higher tax rate. Such talk was most useful to the landowners who took every opportunity to spread the idea. By a decree of August 18, 1785, the government assured the nation that it had no such intention, that the decree was aiming merely at " equitable distribution." [112]

While the project was received with displeasure by the nobility, it was hailed in other quarters as the great act of liberation of the century. " May the Emperor have the courage to carry his plan to perfection," wrote the *Journal de Hervé*, " we dare predict that this epoch will bring to his subjects the Golden Age, the reality of which men have not known hitherto." [113]

110 *Ibid.*, VIII, 69-99.

111 *Ibid.*, VIII, 163.

112 *Ibid.*, VIII, 163-5.

113 P. P. Mitrofanov, *op. cit.*, p. 466.

But difficulties piled up. The survey, which was to have been completed in six months, was still far from concluded when, in February 1787, the Emperor issued a circular in which he " graciously made it known " that it was " very close to his heart, and also highly necessary that the tax regulation be accomplished in all hereditary lands in 1787, in order that the new assessment can surely begin in the year 1788. To this end all means which serve the all-highest interest are to be applied, and all obstacles, be they persons or things, are to be eliminated." [114]

Even among the peasants there was some opposition to the new law, especially on the part of those in the community, the village headmen and elders, who were in charge of carrying it out. A law of December 6, 1787, explained that " agitators and ringleaders who have incited their communities to refuse to give the necessary data . . . are to be punished, with the explanation that the penalty is due solely to their obstinacy." [115]

Unfortunately for the Emperor's plans, the " agitators and ringleaders " reached into the highest quarters. The deputies, whom the Austro-Bohemian Chancellery sent into the province to investigate the situation, agreed that the law would ruin the landowning nobility which, they thought, was " after all much more important to the state than the capitalists [sic!]." [116]

Count Kolowrat, the Vice-chancellor, wrote to the Emperor in a similar tenor.[117] This time Joseph completely lost patience and angrily replied:

All this is empty blabber and superfluous waste of time. These phrases are nothing but ghosts by which one wishes to frighten people and to awaken their dissatisfaction. My principles are unshaken: everyone must pay according to his income . . .

114 *Handbuch, op. cit.*, VIII, 207-8.

115 *Ibid.*, XIII, 219-20.

116 P. P. Mitrofanov, *op. cit.*, p. 468.

117 *Ibid.*, p. 468.

I shall not stoop to investigate what is to the advantage of this or that person. To whoever wins, I wish success with all my heart, just as I regret those who lose under the new regulation.[118]

Kolowrat was not the only target of the Imperial rage. And not all enemies of the scheme got away with merely receiving an angry letter. Three months before the Kolowrat incident, the Emperor had found it necessary to dismiss the head of the *Robot* Abolition Commission, Count Karl Zinzendorf. Zinzendorf was considered an able man, well-versed in economic matters and of generally enlightened tendencies. He was head of the *Hofrechenkammer* (equivalent to a modern ministry of finance) when appointed to the commission and must have seemed admirably fitted for the post. He was also a polite courtier, and it is unlikely that Joseph II ever had any inkling of the venomous hatred with which this shy, quiet and humorless man regarded him. Much of Zinzendorf's dislike for the Emperor was probably personal. In addition he had sacrificed a great deal, including his pietist conscience, in order to achieve a respected position among the Austrian nobility and was therefore loath to see any lessening of the prestige of the aristocracy. Despite these personal reasons, Zinzendorf was one of the few men among Austrian landowners who fought Joseph II for reasons other than self-interest. To Joseph II eventual freedom could be achieved only by a levelling of classes, which to him meant government regulation in the internal sphere and protectionism in foreign trade. Zinzendorf, on the other hand, was not only a free trader, but came close to being an advocate of laissez-faire in internal affairs. His opposition to the Imperial plan was undoubtedly on a much higher level than that of most of the nobles, but he was at one with them in regarding the " liberties of the Estates " as an important aspect of universal freedom. When the interfering state of Joseph II threatened to

118 *Ibid.*, p. 470.

take away one of the most sacred privileges of the nobles by
wiping out the distinction between Church, noble and peasant
land, Zinzendorf was staunchly opposed both to the method
and to the aim of this action. Eventually the Emperor realized,
as the modest count put it later, that " I, with my principles
of honesty, justice and conscientious examination of the facts,
would not let myself be carried away by the impetuosity with
which he wished to overthrow all parts of the administration
without rhyme or reason." [119]

At a session of the commission on February 28, 1788, Zinzendorf defended his opinion as "the cause of truth, order,
and justice." The Emperor, unconvinced, dismissed him. Of
his activities as the president of the commission the count,
speaking of himself in the third person, wrote in his autobiography:

> This burdensome chairmanship, hated by the society in which
> the count lived, the nobility, the count filled with unbelievable
> labor and much vexation from the councillors who were to
> assist him until . . . February, 1788. During this activity
> he repeatedly had to realize that the most important arrange-
> ments were made planlessly, that no one had the patience to
> eliminate difficulties gradually and to win public opinion.
> Impatience, restlessness, great, even beneficient intentions,
> but no desire to think seriously about the means of achieving
> them, these were the defects of the ruler; pride, insolence
> and an envious spirit of independence, those of the *Referenten*
> and councillors. These obstacles made this important chair-
> manship extremely unpleasant for the count. They frustrated
> completely and continually his incessant endeavor to de-
> termine, first, correct and suitable measures and only then
> proceed to their execution. The *cadastre* was rushed, filled
> with contradictions and a failure altogether. Its forcible inter-
> ference with the right of property was entirely unnecessary.

119 Adam Wolf, " Graf Karl von Zinzendorf," *Geschichtliche Bilder aus
Oesterreich*, Vienna, 1878, II, 278.

The count was forced by his conscience to assist diligently in its revocation under the next government.[120]

The chairmanship of the commission, which Zinzendorf had vacated, eventually went to *Staatsrat* von Eger, who was practically the only person upon whose support on the subject of the new tax regulation the Emperor could always count.

The end of objections had not yet come. When the decree was about to be published the Chancellery once more raised its voice in protest. It now begged the Emperor to consider that if the nobles became impoverished, as after the enactment of the decree they surely would, they would no longer be able to support charitable institutions and then continued:

> Holy duty forces the loyal and obedient Chancellery again to lay its view before the all-highest throne. It is, that a decision by authority, which measures all dues by the same scale and commutes them into money payments, without respect for deep-rooted customs, legal contracts, and judicial settlements, is incompatible with the duty of the state to protect its subjects . . . A stroke of the pen is wiping out the right of property which ought to be sacred to the ruler.[121]

Finally they asked that the commutation should at least be postponed until November 1, 1790, in order that the landowners would be able " to find ways and means to comply with this general revolution." [122]

The Emperor answered that the report of the Chancellery was pervaded by " selfishness, self-love " and a desire to make itself popular, but that, since he was not asking for blind obedience, he would answer its arguments. He began by pointing out, perhaps a little facetiously, that those landowners who would suffer damages after receiving the percentage of dues granted to them by the law, must either manage their

120 G. v. Pettenegg (ed.), *Ludwig und Karl von Zinzendorf, ihre Selbstbiographien*, Vienna, 1879, pp. 203-4.

121 P. P. Mitrofanov, *op. cit.*, pp. 639-40.

122 K. Gruenberg, *Bauernbefreiung, op. cit.*, II, 441.

estates very badly or else overburden the peasants. He further stated that the equal distribution of the state's taxes and a reduction of the peasants' payments would lead to a considerable increase in the national wealth and the "whole, horrible revolution would only have the most beneficial consequences." With that harshness which in his later years became characteristic of many of the Emperor's pronouncements he continued: " I am therefore quite calm about its effects, without letting myself be confounded by the noise and grumbling which, in the patriotic tone sung here, is always the consequence, even of the best of measures." [123] The war between the Emperor and his advisers had definitely broken out.

The last incident in the long struggle to publish the regulation occurred on February 5, 1789, five days before the decree was to be announced officially, when Count Rudolf Chotek, the second Chancellor, resigned rather than sign a decree which in his opinion meant the destruction of the nobility. Answering the long letter of resignation in which Chotek had explained his action, the Emperor wrote:

> No matter what steps you may take, I shall not change my action, not even for your sake. I am used to the ingrate, that does not surprise me in the least. But that a man like you should take such a step, solely because of obstinacy and quixotism, does, . . . I must admit, surprise me greatly.

Thus in spite of Chotek, Zinzendorf, Kolowrat, the Council of State and the Chancellery, the decree was published on February 10, 1789. Its preamble announced the completion of the survey of land and the subsequent introduction of a new tax law, designed to " establish that equality which hitherto has been so greatly lacking in the system of taxation." The decree was divided into two parts. The first dealt with

123 *Ibid.*, II, 441.

124 Adam Wolf, " Graf Rudolf Chotek," *Kaiserliche Akademie der Wissenschaften, Sitzungsberichte der Philosophisch-Historischen Classe,* Vienna, 1853, IX, 443.

the Imperial land tax, the second with the subject's payment
to the manorial lord. The new land tax aimed at a " perfectly
equal distribution " by abolishing not only the differences
among estates, but also the quota system for different provinces.[125] Foreseeing that this provision would be much attacked, the law explained:

> The needs of the state, to be covered in part by the produce
> of the land, are proportionately the same in all provinces.
> Therefore the contribution must be the same everywhere and
> no attention paid to the provincial quotas. These, having been
> recognized as faulty are herewith abolished in full.[126]

In the future therefore all those who owned or occupied land,
be they peasants or landowners, were to pay 12 2/9 per cent
of its value in taxes.

Section two of the edict dealt with the peasant's obligations
towards the lord. In the opening paragraph the Emperor declared that it was the final aim of the state " to strengthen
those who live on the land and to enable them to carry out
their duty as citizens." This aim could never be achieved unless the subjects, " severely oppressed by the demands of the
overseers, land, or tithe lords " received relief. He was, Joseph
continued, far from interfering with the property rights of
the nobles; neither did he wish to investigate " those causes,
customs, and contracts, from which the present dues in labor,
money, and kind were derived." But duty which " bound him
to work for the preservation of the whole," forced him to set
" a just goal and irremovable limits " wherever dues and
services surpassed the subject's ability to pay. The subject
should be allowed to keep at least seventy *Gulden* from the
hundred. The remainder was to cover both the land tax and
the obligations to the lord. 12 *Gulden* 13½ *Kreutzer* were to
be devoted to the former and 17 *Gulden* 46⅔ *Kreutzer* to the

125 *Handbuch, op. cit.,* XVII, 152.
126 *Ibid.,* XVII, 154.

latter. These 17 odd *Gulden* were to include money and grain rent, *laudemium, mortuarium,* the tithe, and any other obligation.[127]

The publication of the law was followed by a great outcry. The Estates in the German provinces could not quite rival the indignation of the Galicians or Hungarians although sometimes they came fairly close to it: "The love of truth and justice, which we owe to our fatherland and to your Majesty," wrote the Estates of Styria, " causes us to make these protests." They asked to be allowed to " lay down their respectful objections before the all-highest throne " and then continued:

> If this our humble entreaty, which with an anxious heart, we present to the best, the most gracious and the most just of all monarchs, the father of the fatherland, is rejected, our desperation will know no limits. Terrible need will come over us, we shall be bereft of all we have, our prosperity will disappear, and we shall stand before the eyes of the world as unreliable debtors.[128]

Carinthia, on the other hand, accepted the law with little complaint. It objected only to the subsequent provision that landowners no longer had the privilege of collecting taxes. In that case the Estates felt that they could not be responsible for prompt payments.

Carniola was highly exasperated: " The loyal and obedient Estates deliberated, deliberated for a long time," its representatives wrote to the Emperor, " and the result of these deliberations was the deepest and inmost conviction that the all-highest intentions, if they were directed towards the general welfare, missed their goal."

Even the usually docile Estates of Lower Austria protested mildly against the appointment of Imperial tax collectors. This innovation, they said, deprived them of a right, " acquired

127 *Ibid.*, XVII, 156-70.
128 P. P. Mitrofanov, *op. cit.*, p. 471.

by their constant loyalty, obedience, and devotion to the exalted throne." [129]

These protests had little effect on the Emperor. He made only one minor concession. If a lord found it completely impossible to manage his estate without labor services, the peasants were to perform their customary duties until November 1, 1790. For this work they were to receive a money wage fixed by the government. In other words, the ex-*robot* peasant was to become an agricultural wage-laborer for one year before the full effect of the *robot* abolition system came to fruition. But four months after the enactment of the law, the Emperor died. What was perhaps the greatest single experiment in central European agrarian legislation before the French Revolution was to die with him.

IMPROVEMENTS IN THE PERSONAL LIFE AND MATERIAL ENVIRONMENT OF THE PEASANTRY

General Welfare. The abolition of personal serfdom, the reforms of administration and justice, the innovations in the field of land ownership and inheritance, the " Physiocratic *Urbarium* " were all part of a definite, interdependent and well thought-out plan to free the peasant from dependence on the landowner. Aside from this program, however, Joseph II was very anxious to solve problems arising in the ordinary course of everyday government in a manner beneficial to the peasantry.

Like Maria Theresa he was very much concerned about the health, hygiene, and education of the peasantry and in the main followed the path her measures had shown him.

He paid particular attention to the education of peasant children who, after all, would one day grow up to be what he considered the most important class of his subjects. The difficulties in persuading peasants to let their children go to school were great indeed and all sorts of incentives had to be

129 *Ibid.,* pp. 473-6.

resorted to. Parents were given medals, children new suits of clothes, ceremonies were staged upon such presentations, and a number of new schools were established in rural districts.[130] As children were prevented from attending classes not only by their parents, but sometimes also by the lord's steward who wished to use them for special tasks, the Emperor decreed that "manorial officials were to eliminate all hindrances that prevented children from attending school."[131] Another legal provision affecting school children prohibited principals from accepting into their schools female students wearing a bodice.

The latter provision was part of the war for health and hygiene against the old-fashioned "superstitions" of the people. In the same general category belong the bans on firing shots at weddings and funerals, the abolition of funeral meals, and finally the famous decree on burials which is used so frequently to caricature the reforms of Joseph II that it deserves to be quoted at least in part: "At the burial of the body no other intention can exist than to expedite its putrefaction. Nothing is less suited for this purpose than burial in coffins. Therefore all bodies are to be buried . . . covered only by a linen sack."[132]

This decree aroused so much opposition among the population that it had to be repealed. It is a curious fact, however, that while the law is usually cited as an example of Joseph II's utter lack of understanding for the customs and habits of the people, a failing from which his brother Leopold was admirably free, Arthur Young reports in his Travels that he found the same enactment on his journey through Tuscany.[133]

Actually in both cases the measure was probably designed to save wood. The shortage continued to harass Austrian

130 Handbuch, op. cit., VI, 358-60.

131 Ibid., VIII, 471.

132 Ibid., VI, 565-8.

133 Arthur Young, Travels in the Kingdom of France, Dublin, 1793, pp. 508-10.

society during the reign of Joseph II, although it did not occupy the prominent place in contemporary literature that it did in the time of Maria Theresa.

Little progress was made towards compulsory fire protection. In the main the Emperor limited himself to issuing the customary decrees for the prevention of fire [134] and to directing some expert to write the customary pamphlets on the " fireproofing of building materials at little expense " [135] and similar subjects.

While Joseph II's measures concerning the health and welfare of the population resemble those of Maria Theresa, they differ in one important respect: Maria Theresa had shown an occasional interest in the establishment of insane asylums, poor houses, orphanages and other institutions of that kind, but to Joseph II the matter became a veritable passion. Most of these institutions were a matter of urban development. But the effects of the policy were also felt in the country. Doctors, surgeons, pharmacists and midwives were reminded that they were bound " by the highest laws and by their oath to come to the aid of the truly poor at all times." [136] Food and medicine for poor peasants were provided free of charge, to be paid for by the royal treasury and by the lords. The former were to assume two-thirds, the latter one-third of the burden.[137]

One curious phenomenon, not ordinarily considered characteristic of eighteenth-century rural society, was the occurrence of a considerable number of suicides. Joseph II had little sympathy for those who attempted to take their own lives. His stern sense of duty could not condone so frivolous a shirking of responsibility. Furthermore, every suicide deprived the state of a valuable member. At one time he had a young

134 *Handbuch, op. cit.*, I, 323-41.

135 *Ibid.*, I, 290-99.

136 *Ibid.*, I, 199.

137 *Ibid.*, IV, 18.

man who attempted to kill himself tried for " assault." [138] He
saw his main duty, however, not so much in the punishment
of offenders as in the preservation of lives. He discouraged
the idea, current among the peasantry, that assistance to a
person who had tried to commit suicide brought dishonor,[139]
and issued specific instructions on how those who had attempted to hang or drown themselves were to be revived.

While in its fight against human illness, the government of
Joseph II showed itself somewhat more humanitarian than
the previous regime, it was easily more scientific in the battle
against animal and plant disease. Treatises on the prevention
of such illnesses were still written, but these essays now lost
the rustic tone which had distinguished them in the time of
Maria Theresa and often became dry and scholarly essays, in
search of new methods and materials, full of descriptions of
detailed experiments. They also gave evidence of a geographic
broadening of the horizon of Austrian scientists and scholars.
The early pamphlets had been based almost exclusively on
local Austrian experience, occasionally citing innovations
that the Prussians had found useful in Silesia. In the seventeen eighties, however, it became quite fashionable to
quote non-German examples, particularly French and British
sources.[140]

Hunting Rights. In the agrarian legislation of Joseph II,
the attempt to achieve equality and centralization, the effort
at peasant emancipation rather than peasant protection, is
evident in almost every act. There is, however, one major
exception, the hunting regulation of February 26, 1786. This
law was to supersede all previous legislation on the subject,

138 K. v. Hock and H. I. Bidermann, *op. cit.,* pp. 153-9. The authors blame
the severe treatment of the young man, a noble from a well-known family
and apparently mentally disturbed, on the Emperor's dislike for the nobility.

139 *Handbuch, op. cit.,* I, 162.

140 See, for example, *Beschreibung des Mutterkorns, ibid.,* XIII, 288-94
or Anton Koczian's treatise, *ibid.,* VIII, 366-460.

to be a new and comprehensive code of hunting regulations. The preamble was written in a protective, paternalistic tone more characteristic of Maria Theresa than of Joseph II. It explained that the law was designed not only to protect the peasants against the excesses of the hunter, but also to " preserve to the owners of hunting districts the enjoyment of the rights due to them." Specifically the law provided that wild boars be kept in fenced gardens, and that poachers be punished like ordinary thieves. It also excluded all peasants from the purchase of hunting districts, and therefore from all the privileges of the noble hunter, " since they would only use such an opportunity to neglect their farms and trade." [141] The French Revolution was still far from Austria.

SUMMARY

The reign of Joseph II had been a sad trial for the privileged classes in the Austrian monarchy. He had humbled the nobles by making them one with the " rabble " before the law, by ignoring them socially, by causing them financial losses, and they hated him cordially in return. " Peasant God " they dubbed him, and in their eyes this was the supreme insult. In the first years of his reign this anger had been vociferous but on the whole inactive. But when the continued social reforms, culminating in the abolition of services and the equalization of taxation, threatened to " destroy the great," when the prestige of the Emperor was seriously weakened by his disastrous war against Turkey, when his grave illness foreshadowed a change of government in the near future, the opposition stiffened. A revolt broke out in Belgium, the Hungarians began to negotiate with the King of Prussia, and even in the usually loyal hereditary lands there was unrest and discontent. In addition, the outbreak of revolution in France, the resistance there to the absolutism of the king, encouraged the Austrian nobility who, without fully under-

141 *Ibid.*, XI, 490-502.

standing what was happening in the French capital, borrowed the formal attitudes, if not the spirit of the revolutionaries in Paris. And at the moment when the whole system of reform which he had built up with so much passion and sacrifice came to a crisis, when everything depended on his standing firm, the Emperor died. Had he lived, the fate of Central Europe might have been different and possibly happier.

CHAPTER IV

THE AFTERMATH

THE news of the death of Joseph II brought a sigh of relief to the lips of many an Austrian noble. " That was good of him," Prince Kaunitz is said to have remarked when he heard the news. Undoubtedly his sentiments were widely shared among the aristocracy.

Joseph's successor Leopold, Grand Duke of Tuscany, had long been considered one of the wisest and most prudent princes in Europe. He arrived in Vienna in March 1790, just late enough to escape whatever deathbed instructions his brother might have given him, or any other indentification with the previous regime. Wherever he passed he was besieged with *desideria,* grievances, and petitions by the nobility of the realm, begging him to rectify the damage which the agrarian legislation of his brother had done to the prestige and the property of the aristocracy. The complaints were much the same everywhere. The first and foremost protest was directed against the *Urbarial* Patent of 1789. Then followed in descending order the laws concerning peasant inheritance, the Law Concerning Subjects of 1781, the supervision of penal matters by the local government and finally even freedom of movement of the peasant.

On the tax regulation Leopold gave way almost immediately. The pressure to do so had been tremendous. The obsequies for Joseph II had ended on the 26th of February. On the 27th the Estates of Lower Austria had already assembled to debate the nature of the petition to be sent to Leopold. Ironically enough they asked Count Karl Zinzendorf, one-time head of the tax regulation commission, to draft the document. Only ten days later he read the petition to them, as he has told us in his autobiography, amid great applause.[1]

1 G. von Pettenegg, *op. cit.,* p. 211.

In another four days, two days after Leopold's arrival at Vienna (March 12), the count had already had his first audience with the king, and by a law of March 22, 1790, the tax regulation court commission in Vienna, as well as the various subcommissions in the provinces, were abolished; the supervision of tax and *urbarial* affairs reverted to the provincial government. The same law abolished tax collection by Imperial officials, reasoning that since Imperial tax collectors had to be salaried to fulfill this function, the method meant an additional burden to the peasants. Its abolition was therefore directed towards the "evident relief of the subjects." [2]

THE REPEAL OF THE TAX LAW

Then on April 6, 1790, the first of the decrees abolishing the Josephian tax system was issued. It repealed the law of November 1, 1789 for Lower Austria:

> Immediately at his accession His Majesty, moved by the unanimous complaints of the lords of Lower Austria, and by the discontent of a great many of the subjects themselves, ... decided to make the most thorough investigation of the arrangements concerning the nature and collection of the Imperial land tax and the so-called *urbarial* payments.

The results of this investigation had shown that the system, " far from fulfilling the intentions of His late Majesty," would probably have been abolished even under Joseph, " if all its unfortunate consequences had been as clear at that time as they are today." Leopold's first argument against the new tax system was that the regulation had not worked, that the " main aim of the tax and *urbarial* system, the prosperity of the subjects," had not been achieved. This point, hardly well taken in view of the short time during which the system had been in operation, was followed by what has been called " the most trenchant criticism" of the Josephian tax system:

2 *Sammlung der Gesetze welche unter der glorreichsten Regierung Koenig Leopold II in den Sämmtlichen Erblanden erschienen sind*, Vienna, 1794-96, I, 59-60. This work is hereafter cited as *Sammlung der Gesetze*.

Inexactness of measurement prevailed. Some landowners were allotted more, others less than their true area. Some lands were credited with impossibly high yields, others, to the detriment of their fellow subjects, with much less than their true produce. The cost of transporting grain to the market was completely ignored . . . The so-called parity of all produce with four categories of grain made the registers partly false and partly incomprehensible to the peasants themselves. The assessments are now unequal since no attention was paid to the cost of making land arable . . . A consideration of by-products, as well as of industrial output, which greatly increases the financial standing of the owners of large, and at the same time fertile lands, has been completely neglected.

Leopold further suggested, and in this he has been echoed frequently by later critics, that Joseph had actually put a new burden on the peasants by forcing them to pay their obligations in money when in many instances it would have been easier to fulfill them in kind. This criticism seems rather unfair, for the tax law had clearly stipulated that although henceforth money was to be the measure of all dues, those peasants who found it hard to meet their obligations in currency should be allowed to draw up agreements with their lords to continue paying in kind, as long as these payments did not exceed the 17 7/9 per cent limit set by the law.

In general Leopold's condemnation of the Josephian tax system consisted of a barrage of arguments, some good, some bad, some indifferent, all directed towards the same effort, the denunciation of the " Physiocratic *Urbarium*." In the attempt to achieve this aim, the relative weight and merit of the respective arguments is sometimes lost. For instance, the complaint that, because the *mortuarium* had become part of the percentage of dues to be paid by the peasant, the latter was responsible for his own death tax, appears to be an ingenious but hardly weighty product of a clever legal mind. Equally questionable is the argument that tax collection by Imperial officials, in increasing the expenses of the state, would in the long run increase the burden on the subjects. It is doubtful whether the nobles collected taxes for the love of humanity alone. Whatever the weight of his arguments, Leopold was satisfied that Imperial tax collectors presented a " striking disadvantage " to the subjects. At the same time he considered himself " duty-bound to protect the lawful property of the nobility and to lend an ear to their complaints." For, owing protection to all classes, he could not permit the subjects to " acquire unlawful advantages at the expense of the lords, nor the lords to treat their subjects arbitrarily and illegally." [3]

The state had ceased to be the protector of the peasants. It had again become an arbiter, a referee, meting out meticulous, impartial justice in a struggle in which the opponents compared neither in strength, nor in size, nor in composition, compared in nothing in fact save the assumption of the arbiter that they did compare.

The revocation of the tax law for Lower Austria was followed by a similar law for Austria above the Enns on April 19,[4] for Styria on May 5,[5] for Carinthia on May 20,[6] and for Carniola on June 10, 1790.[7] Thus the "Physiocratic *Urbarium*" was over and done with, and the tax and *robot* systems of Maria Theresa and the early period of Joseph II were restored.

OPPOSITION TO THE REVOCATION OF THE " PHYSIOCRATIC *Urbarium* "

While the nobility had been opposed to the Josephian tax regulation almost *en bloc,* intellectuals and publicists were

3 *Ibid.,* I, 84-96.

4 *Ibid.,* I, 165-78.

5 *Ibid.,* I, 189-203.

6 *Ibid.,* I, 247-60.

7 *Ibid.,* I, 291-304.

of varying opinions. One of the most passionate defenders
of the system was the anonymous author of *Klagen der Unterthanen der Oesterreichischen Monarchie wegen Aufhebung
des Neuen Steuersystems und Wiedereinfuehrung des Alten
[Complaints of the Subjects of the Austrian Monarchy Because of the Abolition of the New Tax System and the Reintroduction of the Old]*. Pretending to be a peasant, he addressed his pamphlet to the Estates in various provinces.
" Worthy fathers of the fatherland," he began, " gracious
lords " :

> Since, by dint of the constitution of each province, you
> alone can represent the people, treat with its imprescriptible
> and inalienable rights, its inviolate and non-transferable lib-
> erties, and protect them against all interference by the royal
> power, . . . duty, which our common mother nature has
> conferred upon us, demands that we, the most numerous part
> of the people, bring before your eyes our grievances and
> melancholy lament . . .

And with what seemed reasonable respect for and confidence
in the honorable men he was addressing, he continued: " Your
justice and love of freedom, whereof at the accession of the
now-reigning king you have given such telling proof, con-
vinces us that you will not only lend an ear to our grievances,
but patriotically take them to heart."

Soon, however, the author's deferential irony gave way
to bitterness and sarcasm. Discussing the sad history of the
peasantry before the reign of Maria Theresa, he wrote: " It
is not unknown to us that, pressed by extortions, weakened
by labor services, embittered by mistreatment they [the
peasants] sometimes made bold to attempt to better their sad,
pitiful lot by rebellion, to break their chains, and that this
punishable audacity always cost bloody heads." Bitterly he
added, " they were always brought to submission by soldiers,
their own sons and brothers, by parricide and fratricide." [8]

8 *Klagen der Unterthanen der Oesterreichischen Monarchie wegen Aufhebung des Neuen Steuersystems*, n. p., 1790, pp. 1-5. This work is hereafter
cited as *Klagen der Unterthanen*.

In due course the author paid his respectful tribute to the agrarian reforms and the good heart of Maria Theresa. But it was Joseph II who was his real hero, and for whom he wrote a eulogy, the glowing tone of which was to become so familiar later in the writings of the enemies of the Metternich System, the polemics of the revolutionaries of 1848:

> Joseph II, the worthy son of the great Theresa, whom we shall never forget as long as a drop of blood flows in our veins, whose name we shall always pronounce with the warmest feeling of gratitude, about whom our children's children will never be able to think except with awe, and with pain at the early death of this rare human being, whose holy ashes we now, since he has passed away to our misfortune, will eternally honor, and at present wish to moisten with our tears, . . . had hardly come to the throne when he held out his fatherly arms to the weak and oppressed and was not afraid to regard the rights of humanity as higher than the privileges, prerogatives, and exemptions of a select few, yes higher even than false glory and wealth.[9]

The Estates, on the other hand, "instead of working for the welfare of the peasantry," thought to "deceive and betray the best of monarchs," the "true father and protector" of the subjects. "Gracious lords," the author exclaimed, "how could you, as defenders and protectors of the rights of the people, say before Joseph, without blushing with shame, that we did not languish in serfdom when you subjected us to its consequences in the most oppressive manner?"[10] Attacking the view held by the nobles that serfdom was the result of ancient contracts between the lords and the subjects, the author contended that such pacts could have been drawn up under two conditions only: either the peasants were not in their right mind at the time, or else they were forced to sign "by fear and threats." In both cases the treaties were invalid, and

9 *Ibid.*, p. 8.
10 Ibid., pp. 10-13.

therefore could not be binding upon the descendants of the original signers. The peasants ought to repudiate such contracts altogether, for the treaties were not only evil in themselves, " an iron chain forged to bind us to the tyranny of the landlord," but " highly detrimental and disadvantageous " to the state as well: " Each private due, paid to vassals of the state, to be dissipated by them in voluptuousness, must necessarily be damaging to the state as a whole, for it decreases the taxes which the subjects are able to pay as citizens to the state." [11]

This, the author thought, the " immortal Joseph " understood well. For these reasons he issued the " Physiocratic *Urbarium*," commuted labor services and established equality of taxation. The charges levelled against the law by the decree of revocation of April 6, 1790, represented merely the private grievances of the nobles and had no bearing on the welfare of either the peasantry or the state as a whole. On the contrary, the peasantry, " by the abolition of the Josephian and the reintroduction of the old barbaric system," had been " handed over to the arbitrary exploitation of the lord and his steward." While the peasantry had paid only thirty *Gulden* from the hundred under the Josephian system, they would now " not even receive the wages of their hard work," as they would have to pay " sixty to seventy *Gulden* purely in *urbarial* dues, and on some manors even more." [12]

The author was no uncritical apologist of the Josephian land survey. He admitted that the survey was inexact in many details, that the cost of transporting grain to the market had been ignored. He felt, however, that these errors could have been corrected without overthrowing the whole plan, that with all its weaknesses the new law was a great improvement over the conditions that had existed before its introduction. The peasantry, he said, had been oppressed for many centuries, had

11 *Ibid.*, pp. 23-4.
12 *Ibid.*, p. 46.

received no really substantial relief until the reign of Joseph
II. Now the new government, deceived by the nobles, proposed
to "force it back into barbarism." This move was not only
cruel, it was unwise. The peasantry had borne its sad lot for
many centuries. But as recent events in France demonstrated,
even its patience did not last forever. The Austrian landowners
would always run the risk of sharing the fate of the French
nobility unless they set aside their selfish interests and became
truly the representatives of the people, the fathers of the
fatherland.[13]

It is difficult to say what the effect of the retention of the
Josephian system would have been. Its inaccuracy as a land
survey is generally admitted. Yet this was merely a weakness
of detail, not of principle, a weakness which the successors of
Joseph II could gradually have corrected, had they had any
desire to do so.

From the point of view of principle the system did have one
serious difficulty. By taxing land and its fertility alone the
Emperor quite wisely refrained from taxing improvements
on the land. But he also refrained from taxing industrial
establishments, thus putting a disproportionate tax burden
on the owners of landed property. From an anonymous
critic in Nicolai's *Allgemeine Deutsche Bibliothek*, 1790,[14] to
Gruenberg a hundred years later, economic writers have
pointed out this weakness.[15] Curiously enough it is also one
of the few features of the "Physiocratic *Urbarium*" that
was retained in Austrian taxation policy into the nineteenth
century.

The basic principle of the whole plan, that of equality of
taxation, was also the feature which was most attacked. It was
revolutionary for the time and the country in which it was
proposed, but it did show foresight and, in the light of sub-

13 *Ibid.*, pp. 131-4.

14 *Allgemeine Deutsche Bibliothek*, Berlin, 1790, XCIII, 255-63.

15 K. Gruenberg, *Bauernbefreiung, op. cit.*, I, 337-8.

sequent events, could probably have been retained, had Leopold and his successors wished to retain it.

The commutation of dues into money payments has seemed to some historians the most important aspect of the whole plan. Grossman, for instance, has held that it was a deliberate attempt on the part of the Emperor to lead Austria from an agrarian to an industrial economy. This policy, he thought, formed the link between Joseph's activity in the agrarian field and his fostering of trade and commerce and thus reconcile the contradiction between " Joseph the Physiocrat " and " Joseph the Mercantilist." The basic contention of his argument is that Joseph II, by freeing the peasants from dues and services, attempted to create a mobile population which would have supplied the labor force to bring about the industrialization of Austria.[16] It is possible that the policies of Joseph II, if allowed to take root, might have had such an effect. On the other hand, it does not seem probable at all that he himself was consciously pursuing such an aim. His ideal, the ideal of most of the " enlightened " statesmen of the time, was still a healthy and prosperous population of small but free peasant owners. It is hardly likely that a peasantry, happy in its rural occupation, would have streamed into urban centers to become factory labor. Indeed, history seems to have provided us with a laboratory experiment in this case. France, where in the Revolution the peasantry was given possession of the land, is to this day largely an agrarian country. On the other hand, enclosures and evictions were necessary to provide laborers for the British factory system.

Joseph II was indeed an inveterate advocate of the expansion of trade and commerce, but believing that a constantly growing population was both possible and desirable, it is hardly likely that he thought that the labor force for these activities would have to be drawn from the ranks of the

16 Henryk Grossmann, " Oesterreichs Handelspolitik," *Studien zur Sozial- Wirtschafts- und Verwaltungsgeschichte*, Vienna, 1914, X, especially vii-viii.

peasantry. Nevertheless, had the Josephian tax law remained in existence, had all lords been forced to pay their laborers in money wages, they might have come to rely more and more on mechanical devices and Austria might have seen industrialization a few decades earlier.

Whatever its weaknesses, the Josephian tax law held within it possibilities of change, of improvement, of progress. It could have been altered; it could have been repealed in part. In any form its provisions would have been preferable to the cumbersome system of dues and services. Its methods may not always have been sound, but the worst that can be said for its philosophy is that it was a little, and very little at that, ahead of its time.

The peasantry was not as convinced as were the nobles and the Emperor that the new system had been to their disadvantage. Riots broke out in various parts of the country where the peasants, after having the burden lifted from them, were again forced to assume their previous obligations. By a resolution of July 9, 1790, Leopold expressed surprise that despite his fatherly concern in repealing the tax law, the peasants had not recognized their own best interest. He was clever enough, however, to understand that little would be achieved by taunting them further. He counselled mildness to the nobility and exercised it himself. Using the time-honored device of fighting rebellion by a combination of blackmail and sweetness, he warned the peasants of the dire consequences which would undoubtedly befall their families if they continued their resistance, but also advised them that he considered their insubordination due mainly to the evil work of ringleaders and agitators and would therefore treat them with fatherly love and forbearance if they mended their ways and became his loving and obedient subjects again.[17] At the same time he sent a sharp warning to the nobles who, relieved of the fear of constant Imperial supervision by the death of Joseph II, had,

17 *Sammlung der Gesetze, op. cit.*, I, 362-5.

in the words of the author of the *Klagen* ... *wegen Aufhebung des Neuen Steuersystems,* " immediately dragged out their rods of punishment and kept them in readiness." [18]

In a letter to the Estates of Lower Austria, Leopold complained that his numerous admonitions had been without avail. By innumerable resolutions, orders and warnings, issued by the local and provincial governments, even by the Estates themselves, the lords, he wrote, had been asked to restrain their stewards and other officials from treating the subjects cruelly. Recent unrest had shown how little these entreaties had been heeded. He " earnestly requested " the lords and their officials " to treat their subjects with all possible mildness, and to refrain from all pettiness, ... at least until the first effervescent rebellion [had] subsided. Action to the contrary [would] only feed resistance and drive the subjects .to actual rebellion." [19]

Leopold, personally, on a visit to Graz, in what he undoubtedly considered a politic move, freed from their imprisonment some of the ringleaders of the peasant revolt in Styria. This amnesty had some unexpected results. The faith of the peasants in the Habsburg Emperors was still such that the rumor gained currency that the agitators had been imprisoned illegally by the " lords spiritual and temporal," while the Emperor was on their side and had set them free as soon as he heard of their predicament. Some of the leaders of the Styrian nobility became very upset about these stories. They had had one Joseph II, they did not want another. Leopold, by a government order of September 11, 1790, denied the rumor publicly and energetically.[20]

LAND OWNERSHIP AND INHERITANCE

In the field of peasant ownership a good deal of the legislation of Joseph II was preserved. In the field of inheritance

18 *Klagen der Unterthanen,* p. 41.

19 *Sammlung der Gesetze, op. cit.,* I, 366-8.

20 *Ibid.,* II, 35-7.

much of it was abrogated. The provisions concerning the mortgaging, sale and exchange of peasant property, the laws on debts contracted by the peasant, as well as those restricting evictions, persisted with little change. On the other hand, in the field of inheritance practically all the laws issued after 1786 were abrogated. With regard to freely inheritable property, peasant inheritance remained the same as that of all other classes. Succession in this case was determined by the provisions of the Josephian Code of Civil Law (*Allgemeines Buergerliches Gesetzbuch*).

Concerning the inheritance of land, the law designating the eldest son as heir remained in force. But while the Josephian law had decided that, if the landlord objected to this heir, the final decision rested with the local government, it was now held that in such cases the second son was to take over the holding.[21]

PRE-EMPTION AND REVERSIONARY RIGHTS

There were few provisions in the reform program of Joseph II that were not attacked by the nobles in that chaotic summer of 1790. One of the more persistent demands was that reversionary right, that old mark of noble distinction, be restored—and in the main the lords had their way. The law for Upper and Lower Austria of December 20, 1790, specified that if a peasant died without an heir his farm was to revert to the lord. In order that the state should not be deprived of all benefits, however, the rest of his estate was to become the property of the government.[22]

The nobility also demanded that the right of pre-emption be restored, but no decision was reached during the reign of Leopold II. The battle continued under the following government and was to become one of the major agrarian issues of the early reign of Francis II.

21 *Ibid.*, II, 165-80.
22 *Ibid.*, II, 290-2.

In order to understand the manner of its solution, it is necessary to consider briefly the personality of Francis II in those early years before he became convinced that the interests of the crown corresponded closely to those of the nobility, before he became one of the cornerstones of the Holy Alliance and, to many, " Metternich's Emperor." As a young man Francis had been brought to Vienna by Joseph II who attempted to instill into his nephew and probable successor his own principles and ideas of government. Joseph was never particularly impressed by his nephew; he questioned his honesty and found that he lacked *ésprit*. Nevertheless Francis had, formally at least, accepted some of his uncle's tenets. We find in him the same petulant dissatisfaction with the inefficiency of government officials. We find also a similar attitude towards peasant emancipation. The Estates ought to recognize, wrote the young crown prince in 1791,

> that the development in rural areas has reached the point where the peasant recognizes the rights he can demand as a human being. He asks to be treated as such. To degrade him again to a beast of burden would have the worst consequences for the Estates themselves.

" It is rather peculiar," he insinuated threateningly, " that the Estates try so hard to eliminate the influence of the sovereign on the rest of the subjects." [23]

In another memorandum of the same year Francis asked Leopold to put a halt to the " general evil, namely the enmity of the different classes, lords, burghers, and peasants toward each other, . . . the unfortunate result of the pride and stupidity of the Estates." " To you," he pointed out to his father, " all classes are equally dear, especially those who contribute most to the welfare of the state . . . None shall suppress the others, but all shall help each other . . .

23 Viktor Bibl, " Die Niederoesterreichischen Staende und die Französische Revolution," *Jahrbuch für Landeskunde Niederoesterreichs*, Vienna, 1903, p. 96.

Our Estates are surprising in their demands, and already have
incurred the hatred of the burghers and peasants. This may
lead to evil consequences." [24]

Given these opinions of the young Emperor, it is not surprising that even under his regime we still find Hofrat von
Kees, an ardent Josephian whom his enemies liked to call a
Jacobin, as the head of the High Court of Justice (*Oberste
Justizstelle*). Von Kees was still able, in a resolution which
reads like a summary of the agrarian philosophy of Joseph II,
to refuse to recommend the reintroduction of the right of pre-
emption:

> The soil is the only wealth of the peasant. He can contribute
> to the tax and conscription systems only according to the
> extent and fertility of the land he owns. So long as the lord
> has a right of pre-emption, the property of the peasant is
> never secure. The landowner need only cast a covetous
> glance on this or that piece of land and his steward will un-
> doubtedly find ways and means to flatter the peasant out of
> it, force him to give it up, or even evict him.[25]

If, as the Estates claimed, Kees continued, the absence of
the right of pre-emption would prevent the growth of the
nobility, this would be a small loss to the state since the aristocracy had at any rate grown too fast in proportion to the rest
of the population, and since, moreover, " origin has no influence upon industry, skill and honesty, the true values of the
human being." [26] And again, characteristically, he concluded
by saying that land was after all used much more profitably in
the hands of the peasantry than in the hands of those " who
often never set a foot on their estate for years, leave their subjects to the mercy of some steward or tenant, and consume its
yield in the capital." To this statement the Estates replied in-
dignantly that Kees had slandered them by presenting them

24 *Ibid.*, p. 96.
25 *Ibid.*, p. 94.
26 *Ibid.*, p. 94.

"as a useless burden, created solely to consume the sweat of the subjects in the capital." [27] But neither their shocked anger nor their unattractive metaphor saved the right of pre-emption.

JUSTICE AND SERFDOM

In the field of justice the successors of Joseph II retained much of his legislation. Leopold fought hard and successfully to preserve the Law Concerning Subjects and the Penal Law of 1781. The outstanding position of the *Untertansadvocat* as protector of the peasants was also maintained in all provinces except Tyrol, where the office was abolished by a decree of April 6, 1791, as "not being in conformity with the constitution of the land Tyrol." [28] Neither was Leopold willing to drop the educational qualification for judges which his brother had instituted or to give preference to noble candidates for judicial offices. In answer to grievances of the Estates of Styria with regard to the administration of justice, he made it quite clear that he reserved for himself the privilege of filling judicial offices with capable men, regardless of their birth or rank: "A pure, irreproachable administration of justice," he wrote, "is the first duty of the monarch." He added sarcastically that it would be "very agreeable to him if the qualities necessary for judicial posts would be found especially among the members of the aristocracy competing for such offices." [29]

Leopold would not listen either to the complaints made against the abolition of serfdom, or more specifically against its most important feature—freedom of movement. Soon after his accession he expressedly confirmed the provisions Joseph II had made and later even extended the freedom of movement of the peasant: "Our attention, directed towards the general welfare," he wrote, "combined with our all-highest inclination to give at all times proofs of our fatherly love to our hereditary

27 *Ibid.*, p. 95.

28 *Sammlung der Gesetze, op. cit.*, III, 302-6.

29 H. J. Bidermann, "Die Verfassungskrisis im Steiermark," *Mitteilungen des Historischen Vereines fuer Steiermark*, Graz, 1873, XXI, 46.

lands, has prompted us to extend to emigrants to Hungary the patent of March 14, 1785, concerning freedom of movement and fees on departure." [30]

ADMINISTRATION

In the field of public administration the developments were in a sense most interesting in that they were symptomatic of the whole struggle. For, if the Estates were restored to the privileged position they had enjoyed before the accession of Maria Theresa, whatever Leopold could save of the reforms of " enlightened absolutism " in other fields, would undoubtedly eventually be snowed under in the resurgence of the old feudal spirit. His attitude in the matter was typical of his character. Outwardly he gave in immediately. The regular assembly of the estates came back, its standing committee was again separated from the executive and restored to its pre-Josephian size. In the chambers of the Estates of Lower Austria a truly touching scene is said to have taken place when the Imperial rescript restoring the " liberties " of the nobles was read; we are told that " tears of unlimited awe and of sublime thankfulness ran down the cheeks of the whole numerous assembly." [31]

Yet Leopold had no intention of letting the actual administrative functions fall back in the hands of the Estates, and steadily refused demands that the local governments become attached to the Estates. On the contrary, he sharply declared that he had "deigned to decide " that the local governments should remain an " agency of the Imperial administration alone, dependent solely on the provincial government." [32]

The negotiations about the restoration of the constitution of the Estates in Styria were marked by a curious episode: The peasantry tried to enter the Assembly of the Estates. Although the attempt was unsuccessful, the actions and speeches

30 *Sammlung der Gesetze, op. cit.*, IV, 350-1.

31 V. Bibl, *op. cit.*, p. 79.

32 *Sammlung der Gesetze, op. cit.*, III, 345-6.

which the subject evoked throw a good deal of light upon the position of the peasantry in the German provinces of the Habsburg monarchy at the end of the eighteenth century.

The occasion for this move arose when the towns tried to extend their representation, which consisted solely of the town marshall (*Staedtemarschall*) who had "the more ridiculous than glorious task of representing thirty-one Styrian towns and market places in the provincial diet, that is to vote in their name, and to speak if the nobility and the clergy granted him that privilege." [33] The towns sent a letter to Vienna, asking for additional votes in the Styrian Diet. Their petition was discussed in the so-called court conference, which under Francis II began to replace the more formal meetings of the Council of State. During these discussions the *Referent* von Waidmannsdorf suggested that the peasants should also be represented in the provincial assembly. His views were supported by Hofrat von Kees who characteristically declared that, while the Estates were in theory the representatives of the people, they represented at present in all their three sections only one interest, that of the landowner.[34] With this argument, however, Kees had handed to his adversaries the weapon they needed. Count Rudolph Chotek, whose deep faith in the "liberties" of the Estates had been proved by his dramatic refusal to sign the Josephian tax law, declared that, while he was by no means opposed to the admission of burghers into the assembly, he was in complete disagreement with the opinion that the Estates were the representatives of the people. Kees had put the argument fallaciously, he said. He should not have said, "the Estates are the representatives of the people and therefore the burghers are part of them," but "the Estates ought to be the representatives of the people and therefore the burghers ought to be part of them." If one were to accept the correctness of the second proposition, it would undoubtedly

33 H. J. Bidermann, "Die Verfassungskrisis im Steiermark," *op. cit.*, p. 32.

34 *Ibid.*, p. 41.

follow that the peasantry ought to be represented in the assembly as well. But what would be the consequences of such a move, the count asked in dismay: " What if those to whose advantage one wishes to apply this sentence will not be content with such demands as the public administration is willing to satisfy? What if, after having been admitted legally against the will of the nobility and of the clergy, they will press for a method of representation more in accord with the arithmetic number of the population? What if they gradually dislodge the privileged estate completely and desire to replace it by a truly democratic representation?" [35] This reference to the events in France sufficed. The peasantry did not enter the Estates of Styria.

THE COMMUTATION OF SERVICES

" By two great reforms," wrote Heinrich Friedjung, " Joseph II has earned the gratitude of the peasants of his Empire: by abolishing serfdom (bondage to the soil) in 1781 and by decreeing that even those peasants who did not have full property rights could no longer be evicted." [36] These reforms as well as much of the Emperor's legislation in the fields of administration and justice remained intact, and continued to function, although not always in their original form, until the Revolution of 1848. On the other hand, he had failed completely and utterly to abolish labor services. As long as these existed, all other efforts towards the emancipation of the peasants remained half measures at best. For the next sixty years, to all those concerned with the problems of the peasantry, the question of services was to become an issue of overwhelming importance beside which all others dwindled into insignificance.

Leopold II had given up all attempts to force a legal and compulsory commutation of dues into money payments.

35 Chotek's opinion is reprinted, *ibid.*, pp. 78-81.

36 Heinrich Friedjung, " Freunde und Gegner der Bauernbefreiung in Oesterreich," *Historische Aufsätze*, Stuttgart, 1919, p. 40.

Nevertheless he was convinced that the principle itself was a good one and was anxious to see contracts of commutation drawn up by voluntary agreements between the lords and the peasants. By the patent of April 6, 1790, he reminded the Estates that they had declared themselves willing to " come to an amicable agreement " with their peasants if the latter had other occupations and would find it easier to pay in money than in labor. "The completion of such negotiations," he wrote, " by a voluntary agreement between lords and subjects would arouse our greatest pleasure." [37] Joseph already had exempted all commutation contracts from the documentary tax. Leopold extended this principle by exempting all contracts converting the tithe into money payments.[38]

The government's main expert on agrarian affairs in this period was still *Hofrat* von Eger who, although a Josephian body and soul, was in very good standing with the Emperor Leopold. After the death of Leopold, the struggle within the government between the Josephian faction, of which Eger and Kees were the most outstanding members, and the more conservative officials continued. Eger, to whom labor services were " a grave critical illness from which the whole body politic was suffering," conceived of a new plan for their commutation. The nobles (for the moment in Lower Austria only) were to draw up contracts with their peasants. The local governments were to inspect these contracts and to decide on a fair monetary equivalent for the peasant's obligations. The commutation itself was to be compulsory. The plan, while similar in idea to the project of Joseph II, was designed to pay greater attention to local conditions and problems and was therefore thought fairer to both peasants and owners than the sweeping generalizations of the " Physiocratic *Urbarium*."

Francis II had already consented to the execution of Eger's project when First Chancellor Count Kolowrat, Count Hatzfeld, and other members of the inner court circle warned

37 *Sammlung der Gesetze, op. cit.*, II, 17.

38 *Ibid.*, I, 84-96.

him of the fearful consequences which would most surely result from so revolutionary a move. The whole province, they said, would be filled with unrest, the peasants would stop working completely for they would always expect further relief, and finally the nobility would be plunged into despair.[39] In the end Francis was convinced. The idea of complsory commutation was abandoned.

From this moment the whole tenor of the debates changed. No longer were the discussions primarily concerned with the principle of compulsory commutation, but rather with the problem of whether the central government ought to lay down rules for such commutation as did take place. These negotiations became especially acute around the middle of the decade when most of the commutation contracts which had been concluded during the last years of the reign of Joseph II, or right after the repeal of his tax law, were about to expire. In the court conference Eger fought with great tenacity for the principles of Joseph II, for his own, for the whole idea of the enlightenment—and lost. It was only too easy to show the spiritual kinship between his principles and those of the mortal enemy across the Rhine. Count Karl Zinzendorf, the old foe of commutation, expressed the prevailing feeling among the upper classes well when he said sardonically:

> The landowner has a full legal right to the services of his subjects. This right has been publicly and solemnly recognized. The subjects, if they do not reach an amicable settlement with their lords, must again perform services. Week work, however, might arouse the displeasure of the subjects. Therefore, one wishes to make regulations for their benefit, regardless of laws and solemn promises, and to ignore private rights for the security and welfare of the whole . . . These are highly dangerous principles![40]

39 Viktor Bibl, "Das Robot-Provisorium fuer Niederoesterreich," *Jahrbuch für Landeskunde Niederoesterreichs*, Vienna, 1905, p. 240.
40 *Ibid.*, p. 250.

To these legal considerations *Hofrat* Geisslern added a practical one. It was an objection to peasant emancipation which had been generally raised by the nobles from the beginning, but had usually been ridiculed by Imperial officials. That it was now brought up by one of the latter is a good indication of how, under the influence of the revolution in France, the intellectual climate had begun to change. " The government," he said, " should keep the subjects in that constant activity and industry without which they, as an idle or insufficiently occupied class of human beings, frequently endanger the inner tranquillity of the state." By the abolition of labor services the " work, assiduity and industry " of the subjects would be reduced and the state would have to contend with idle subjects who " not infrequently endanger its safety." [41] The debate was wound up by the words of old Count Kolowrat who said: " For quite some time there have been few complaints about labor services. Therefore, considering present circumstances, it is better to do nothing than to give cause for new complaints and discontent by publishing regulations." [42]

With these words the count had delineated the dominant political philosophy in Austria for the next fifty years. In a resolution to the Emperor the majority recommended that " labor services should not be abolished generally *ex imperio*, but that individual commutations should be left to voluntary agreements between lords and subjects." [43]

This principle became law by the decree of September 1, 1798,[44] euphemistically called a law of " free bargaining " between lords and subjects. It was, however, if we consider the strength of the contending parties, neither free nor bargaining. With it ended half a century of agrarian reform in Austria. In the seventeen-forties the government had entered the field as the champion of the peasants, now it withdrew: The spirit of Joseph had given way to the spirit of Metternich.

41 *Ibid.*, pp. 262-3.
42 *Ibid.*, p. 273.
43 *Ibid.*, p. 273.
44 K. Gruenberg, *Bauernbefreiung, op. cit.*, II, 478-9.

CHAPTER V
LATER PERSPECTIVES

IF we ask why a peasantry which had seen the promised land of reduced dues and services accepted so meekly the return of its old burdens, various answers suggest themselves. The most obvious one is perhaps that the Josephian reforms had had little time to establish themselves. They had been gifts from above rather than the satisfaction of demands from below, their duration had been much too short for them to become part of the way of life of a peasantry whose mode of existence had changed little for centuries and whose minds could not conceive of a future very different from that past. Those among the intellectuals and the bureaucracy who spoke for its welfare were, as we have seen, seriously hampered by the spiritual kinship between their ideas and the principles preached by the hostile armies of the French Revolution and the Napoleonic Empire. In addition, the continual wars in which Austria was involved proved a great pacifier of internal troubles and made the relationship between landowners and peasants for the time being a matter of secondary importance.

FOREIGN OBSERVERS

What remained in the Austria of Francis II of the reforms of Maria Theresa and Joseph II made, in the opinion of many, the Austrian peasant, at least in the hereditary lands, one of the most fortunate of his class in Europe.

" Here in the Austrian monarchy," wrote Stein to a friend from his exile in 1809,

> infinitely more has been done for the peasant than in Prussia, even by the Edict of October 9, 1807. Bondage to the soil was abolished on November 1, 1781, as were all grain and mill restrictions. Only those concerning liquor licenses remained. In each district lawyers for the peasantry are employed. With the exception of Hungary and Galicia, the

peasants are owners. Your honor will realize how backward Prussian agrarian legislation is compared to the Austrian.[1]

" The condition of the peasantry in this monarchy," the emancipator of the Prussian peasants wrote to another acquaintance, " is much happier than in Prussia." Personal servitude, he continued, had been abolished, royal domains divided up, a large number of the peasants had acquired rights of ownership, mill restrictions no longer existed, and government lawyers represented the rights of the subjects against the lords free of charge. " Read," he added, " the laws of Joseph II and of Francis II and you will find the proof of these assertions." [2]

Sismondi in *Nouveau Principes d'Economie Politique* wrote in a similar vein. He even saw in the reforms of Maria Theresa and Joseph II the reason why Austria had not fallen victim to the French Revolution, why, during all the international wars in which the Habsburg Empire had been involved, the peasantry, far from using the dire situation of the government to its own advantage, had clung loyally to the Imperial house. Analyzing the agrarian reforms of Maria Theresa and Joseph II, he was particularly impressed by the fact that under Austrian law nobles could not acquire peasant land. As a consequence of this prohibition, he said, the rural population was enjoying " abundance and security." " The Austrian government," he continued

> by coming to the aid of a class which, if left to itself would necessarily be oppressed, has compensated by the happiness of its subjects . . . for the majority of the vices of its system. In a land deprived of liberty, where finances have always been badly administered, where wars are eternal and disastrous, the great mass of people, consisting almost solely of peasant proprietors, live in comfort and have been made happy; and that

1 Erich Botzenhart (ed.), *Freiherr vom Stein, Briefwechsel, Denkschriften, Aufzeichnungen*, 7 vols., Berlin, 1931, III, 151.

2 *Ibid.*, III, 150.

mass of subjects, knowing their good fortune and resisting all change, have frustrated every project of revolution and every plan of conquest directed towards that empire.[3]

Apparently even Napoleon himself thought that there was much that was interesting and instructive in the agrarian activity of Joseph II. During his sojourn in Vienna after the Battle of Austerlitz he called Count Karl von Zinzendorf for an interview. The main topics of conversation, the count has related, were the economic reforms of Joseph II and the fact that the *cadastre* in France had already cost the Emperor six million francs.[4]

The well-being of the Austrian peasantry was also confirmed by observers less conscious of the political implications of their testimony. An English traveler, Sir Richard Hoare, wrote on a visit to Styria during the last decade of the eighteenth century that " throughout the whole of this country the industry of the peasantry is agreeably conspicuous, . . . on the very summits of mountains I could descry small plots of cultivated land." [5]

Marcel de Serres, on the other hand, preparing a geographic, economic, and statistical survey of the Austrian monarchy for the benefit of the French army of occupation during the years 1809 and 1810, was less impressed by the advances made by Austrian agriculture. " The various branches of rural economy," he wrote, " are still, in many provinces of the Austrian monarchy, far from having attained the perfection of which they are capable." He attributed this circumstance partly to the difficulties of communication due to the dispersion and great distances between estates, partly to the bad example set by municipal and royal domains, but above all

3 J. C. L. de Simonde de Sismondi, *Nouveau Principes d'Economie Politique*, 2 vols., Paris, 1827, II, 210-11.

4 Adam Wolf, " Graf Karl von Zinzendorf," *op. cit.*, p. 301.

5 Sir Richard Hoare, *Recollections Abroad During the Years 1788, 1789, 1790*, Bath, 1815, p. 104.

to "the ignorance of the inhabitants of the country."[6] "The reforms of Joseph II," he wrote, "failed because the views of the Emperor were too advanced for the century in which he lived and particularly for the nation he had been called upon to govern."[7]

Serres thought that Austrian agriculture had profited little by the innovations of Joseph II. The rural population had derived the greatest benefit not from conscious agrarian reform, but rather from the indirect workings of the government's monetary policy. The introduction of paper money, its rapid increase, and the attendant rise of prices, had greatly increased the value of landed property and at the same time decreased the purchasing power of money. Therefore, "many a bearer of an illustrious name" had seen himself forced to stay at home and cultivate his estates. In addition, "the abuse to which paper money had been put, as well as its enormous increase, has caused most of the great capitalists to put their funds in land." This interest in real estate by the leaders of industry, Serres thought, would eventually lead to the application of capitalist methods in agriculture, and therefore "increase the productivity of farms and estates."[8]

The "enormous increase in paper money," however, led to consequences less favorable than investment in land by great capitalists—the state bankruptcy of 1811.

THE *Vormärz* PERIOD, 1815-1848

As a result of the bankruptcy many of its victims seem to have been forced to sell their estates. Frequently the new owners were ignorant of the obligations of the peasant, and when they demanded the old dues and services the peasants refused to perform them, or performed them only in part. The

6 Marcel de Serres, *Voyages dans l'Empire d'Autriche*, 4 vols., Paris. 1814, I, 435.

7 *Ibid.*, II, 19.

8 *Ibid.*, I, 436.

confusion created by such occurrences, as well as the sad state of government finance, led the central administration to attempt to find a new and fairer method of taxation. The amount of taxes due from any individual was now to be based on his net instead of his gross income. Immediately difficulties began to appear. Should the subjects be allowed to subtract their *urbarial,* tithe, and other obligations from their gross income? Although there was a great deal of discussion on this issue, no definitive action was taken. By a provisional decree all regulation was delayed until a new land survey had taken place. This survey was not completed until 1843 when, in spite of the protests of the Estates of Lower Austria, the government decided that it was best for the tranquillity of the country to disregard the survey and to forget about the projected tax regulation. The government was not unaware that its financial difficulties were closely bound up with the persistence of dues and services. But, like the Emperor Francis, it considered labor services a " school of obedience and humility " [9] and was loathe to interfere with the " well-earned property rights " of the nobles. Therefore little changed in the legal status of the Austrian peasant in the *Vormärz* period. Those who read contemporary descriptions on the subject, like the article on the peasantry in the *Oesterreichische Nationalencyclopedie* published in 1835, will find little or nothing that would not have been equally valid in 1790.[10] While the position of the Austrian peasantry may have been more fortunate than that of most of its neighbors in 1790 or even in 1810, by the eighteen-thirties or forties the latter had largely caught up with or even overtaken it.

The question of the commutation or abolition of labor services was not again taken up until the peasant uprising in Galicia in 1846 frightened both the government and the nobility and prompted the former to take some action. Based

9 Viktor Bibl, *Kaiser Franz,* Leipzig, 1936, p. 298.
10 J. Czikam and F. Gräffle (eds.), *op. cit.,* pp. 205-207.

on suggestions by Count Pillersdorf, one of the more liberal members of the government, a law was issued on December 18, 1846. It is said to have contained little that could be applied successfully to the situation and had almost no practical effect.

Essentially the attitude of the Austrian government on the agrarian question was clear and, from its own point of view, understandable. The liberals, the nationalists, were creating enough problems. The government had no intention of adding to its own difficulties by stirring up agrarian unrest as well. As history had shown, the peasantry was no danger to the Austrian state. It would never think of rising unless the impetus for such a revolt were given by outside forces, by the liberals, by the nationalists, by the government itself. The words of Count Kolowrat in 1798 had been wise ones: " It is better to do nothing than to give cause for new complaints and discontent by publishing regulations."

This fear of change, however, made the government so conservative that even the nobles became radical by comparison. A considerable faction of the aristocratic opposition had changed colors since the days of Joseph II and, led by the more liberal section of the Estates of Lower Austria, had turned into a party of moderate reform. Their most effective spokesman was perhaps one Baron Andrian-Werburg who thought that liberty and progress could best be realized in a restoration of the life and vigor of the estates, which, deprived of their powers by the blows dealt to them by enlightened absolutism, had been made entirely apathetic by the unenlightened and bureaucratic absolutism of the existing regime (1841). A revival would be accomplished only by allowing burghers and peasants to enter the estates on an equal footing with the nobility and clergy. Despite this political equality which Andrian was willing to accord to the peasantry, he was careful to preserve the economic privileges of his fellow nobles: " The special relationship between landowners and peasants which still exists in several provinces would not be disturbed in the least by the emancipation of the communities—all dues and services in money and kind, which the peasants have been obliged to pay or perform hitherto, will naturally be preserved most carefully." [11] A logical outcome of Andrian's position was that he could not blame the sorry state of Austrian agriculture on labor services as did most other critics. He attributed it rather to the faulty system of taxation which hit " the main source of national wealth, agriculture, so disproportionately," but hardly touched any other income.[12]

In his main tenets Andrian presented a complete antithesis to the views of Joseph II and his followers. Where Joseph II had attempted to free the individual from all class and corporate loyalties, Andrian attempted to resurrect these loyalties in a fairer but also more rigid manner. Where Joseph II had attempted to abolish dues and services, Andrian wished to preserve them scrupulously. Where Joseph II wanted to tax the fertility of the soil alone, Andrian would have shifted the tax burden almost completely to industry and commerce.

Andrian's views did not go unchallenged. They were attacked with particular vehemence by the anonymous author of *Oesterreichs Innere Politik*: " Boldly and audaciously," he said of Andrian's work,

has this book thrown away the mask which so long has covered aristocratic tendencies. We look upon the unveiled face. It is well known as that of the medieval feudal despot and rebel vassal, surrounded by the flames of glowing red anger because the plans of his party have not yet been realized.[13]

As against this medieval despotism the author felt himself the heir of two other systems, those of Maria Theresa and Joseph II. By them, he explained, " the people have been

11 Viktor von Andrian-Werburg, *Oesterreich und dessen Zukunft*, Hamburg, 1843, p. 158.

12 *Ibid.*, p. 115.

13 *Oesterreichs Innere Politik*, Stuttgart, 1847, p. 20.

raised in a most humanitarian fashion and completely freed from the slavish dependence upon the upper classes." [14]

Turning to the peasantry in particular, the author deplored the revocation of the tax system of Joseph II. " The services, the tithes, and other obligations of that nature," he wrote, " burden the peasant most." [15] Asking himself why so little had been done for the peasantry since the " glorious days of Joseph II," he concluded that since that time it had " only had enemies in the salons of the aristocracy."

> This could not remain without effect on the bureaucracy, for it could least of all expose itself to the suspicion of demagogy. The friends of the people are in the aristocratic view the enemies of the state. This is only natural as the nobles consider the state as an institution created for their benefit and the people as cows destined to be milked by them to the last drop. Whoever does not agree with them incurs the hatred of this mighty party and will be grimly persecuted by it. This is even today the fate of Joseph II, whose exalted character they have slandered and torn down in an unbelievably poisonous fashion. To complete the farce, they have even denied his creative spirit and the great talent of organization which distinguished him, and have placed him in the category of intellectually limited and useless monarchs. If the ruler is slandered simply because he was a friend of the people, how would they have treated any man who had risen from the midst of the people and represented their interest.[16]

Our author, however, not to be frightened, suggested a program of agrarian reform which had all the ear-marks of being patterned on the political philosophy of Maria Theresa and Joseph II. His plan for the commutation or abolition of labor services resembled somewhat the project which Eger had suggested to Francis II in the seventeen-nineties. The

14 *Ibid.*, pp. 1-3.
15 *Ibid.*, p. 78.
16 *Ibid.*, p. 78.

nobles would be forced to commute services if the peasants demanded it, the details of the agreement being left to the discretion of the local government.[17] The author, like Joseph II before him, was opposed to the divisibility of peasant land because the " sorry result of divisibility " was " great impoverishment " which would force many to emigrate.[18] He advocated the reduction of holidays and the abridgment of the control of the clergy over the morals and education of the peasantry.[19] In all these fields, he thought, great progress had been made during the reigns of Maria Theresa and Joseph II, but since that time everything had fallen into neglect. Eventually he gave his reasons why the state should help the peasantry, reasons which were closely akin to the philosophy of enlightened absolutism in Austria:

> The peasantry will at all times form the natural counterweight to the aristocracy and its encroachments. The nobles have never been able to draw the peasants within the circle of their interests and never will. But the government should be able to count on the peasantry in any emergency and should allay any doubts about the side upon which the peasantry will range itself in time of conflict, otherwise it faces incalculable danger. This great truth must overcome all objections against peasant emancipation, whatever may be their nature.[20]

Summarizing his impressions of the agrarian situation in Austria, he wrote:

> Theresa's and Joseph's reforms concerning the relationship between landowners and peasants had not yet reached their aim when these rulers left the scene of their activity. Their successors, the Emperors Leopold and Francis, accepted the conservative principle of government and therefore had to

17 *Ibid.*, p. 87.
18 *Ibid.*, p. 79.
19 *Ibid.*, p. 101.
20 *Ibid.*, p. 93.

drop the reforms altogether. Hence a problem which should have been solved seventy years ago is still awaiting its solution.[21]

A feeling that Maria Theresa and Joseph II had started a task which still needed completion was general among more liberal political thinkers. The fact that Joseph II had been much closer to achieving this aim than the *Vormärz* government, added a great deal to this sentiment. This view was found especially among the members of the lower bureaucracy. When Kuebeck was still a minor official with one of the local governments, and not yet Metternich's chief financial adviser, he had written that, the more he studied agrarian conditions, the more certain he was that the system could not endure without change. The Emperor Joseph, he continued,

> had, either because he held the same view, or else because he had political reasons, begun his immortal work. By the regulation of the land tax he had broken the special relationship between owners and peasants. At the accession of the Emperor Leopold the nobility succeeded in persuading this monarch to revoke the work of the Emperor Joseph. But they could not undo it completely. It lives in the memory of the peasants, is handed down from father to son to grandson, and will eventually again become a reality.[22]

Kuebeck was no uncritical admirer of the "Revolutionary Emperor." He was too greatly influenced by the atmosphere of "legitimacy and compensation" around him to be able to approve whole-heartedly of Joseph's "radicalism." Yet he could see no solution to the agrarian problem except Joseph's:

> To resort to these measures was bold and spiteful, for they were despotic. But to preserve them would have been easy for those who had no part in their creation and did not share

21 *Ibid.*, pp. 5-6.

22 Max von Kuebeck (ed.), *Die Tagebuecher des Karl Friedrich Freiherrn Kuebeck zu Kuebau*, 2 vols., Vienna, 1909, I, 93.

the stain of their spite. Their revocation was a weak mistake, unfortunate for the nation and for the reigning house.[23]

If he himself, he speculated, should ever be called upon to act legislatively in the matter, he would " follow the direction of the Emperor Joseph since it was consonant with the true state of affairs," but would attempt not to injure the rights of property. And prophetically he concluded that " that which the Emperor Joseph had already achieved will sooner or later, but perhaps with convulsions and dangers, again return to life." [24]

It was not an accident that Kuebeck was relating the story of the reforms of Joseph II as if it were something new and unknown. Francis II had realized early in his reign that much of the praise of his late uncle was a barb directed against his own government. And while it was impossible and incompatible with the dignity of the Imperial house to prohibit all laudatory references to the late Emperor, the censors were directed not to allow the printing of works discussing the reforms of Joseph II in detail. This deliberate secrecy on the part of the government about the social and economic history of Austria may in good part explain the " impractical " and " visionary " qualities for which the Austrian liberals of 1848 have so often been reproached. Hans Kudlich, who in 1848 was to introduce into the Reichstag the bill emancipating the peasantry, has told in his autobiography how he and other select members of his class had to meet clandestinely with one of the more liberal of their professors, the economist von Holger, in order to be " initiated into the secret principles of the Josephian reforms." [25]

Unfortunately for the government, its policy backfired. In the end not only the opposition, but the government as well,

23 *Ibid.*, I, 93.

24 *Ibid.*, I, 93.

25 Hans Kudlich, *Rueckblicke und Erinnerungen*, 3 vols., Vienna, 1873, I, 24.

was without exact knowledge of agrarian conditions. Kuebeck in his autobiography has related the following conversation between the Emperor Francis, Count Kolowrat, head of
the political section of the Council of State, and himself. Kolowrat deplored the state of *robot* affairs and thought that
something had to be done about it:

> Emperor: "What? Shall we force the people? Is not
> everyone free to come to an agreement with his
> subjects?"
> Kolowrat: "I beg your pardon, such commutations are now
> prohibited."
> Emperor: "I know nothing of such a prohibition, Kuebeck
> shall inform us about the matter."

Kuebeck added that he had to agree with the Emperor,
there was no such prohibition.[26]

If Kolowrat, who after Metternich was the most powerful
person in the Austrian monarchy, and in internal affairs probably more influential and certainly more interested than the
Chancellor, could make so elementary a mistake, the censorship must really have done its work well. What could be more
typical of the whole situation than that the only intellectual
activity in which Austria really excelled in the *Vormärz* period
was lyrical poetry.

Not that the poets and dramatists were entirely indifferent
to the iniquities of the Metternich system. Grillparzer, Lenau,
Bauernfeld, Hartmann, and above all Anastasius Gruen (Anton Alexander Count Auersperg) attacked it frequently and
often savagely. In the poem *Zinsvoegel* (Rent Birds) Gruen,
himself a descendant of one of the most powerful aristocratic
families in Austria, assailed the system of dues and services
to which the peasantry was still subject. He described how a
peasant, driving his full wagon home from the fields, was
waylaid by an eagle, a falcon, and a raven, each demanding
a part of his harvest for services they claimed they were render-

26 Max von Kuebeck (ed.), *op. cit.*, I, 537.

ing to him. The first maintained that he protected the chicken of the farmer by hiding it in his stomach, the second that he, not the sun or rain, had made the seeds grow, and the third that he would finally outlive the peasant and bury him. The peasant, deprived of the produce of his labor, lay down to sleep, praying that one day God would help him shoot the eagle, catch the falcon in a sling, and twist the neck of the raven. The poet concluded by vouching for the authenticity of the conditions he described: " This song," he wrote, " is sung by one of the race of the falcons, who has often carried home his food from the harvest wagon, and, God knows, he did not like it." [27]

Gruen's hero, the hero of most of the poets and writers who were at war with the " antidiluvian system of Prince Metternich " [28] was Joseph II. To the men of the *Vormärz* period the " Revolutionary Emperor " came to stand for all that the present government did not—peasant emancipation, freedom of the press, tolerance, healthy, active, energetic state activity. To the poet Bauernfeld, Saladin in Lessing's *Nathan the Wise* even appeared as a " sort of Turkish Emperor Joseph." [29]

It is clear that from these men we cannot expect a cool analysis of the Emperor's work. Such writings would at any rate hardly have emerged from the censorship office. What we do find is poetry full of enthusiasm and vigor, fighting a good fight for freedom, honor, love, humanity against cruelty, tyranny, stupidity and sloth. In this struggle Joseph II was the guardian angel, and as such he entered the Revolution of 1848.

27 Anastasius Gruen, " Zinsvoegel," *Der Oesterreichische Vormaerz,* Leipzig, 1931, p. 277.

28 Franz Grillparzer in a poem entitled "Antediluvianisch " had written:
Frueh, eh die Flut noch in die Welt gebrochen,
Gab es Geschoepfe ob zwar wunderlich
Des zeugen noch fossile Mammutknochen
Und das System des Fuersten Metternich.

29 Eduard Bauernfeld, *Erinnerungen Aus Alt-Wien,* Vienna, 1923, p. 9.

The Revolution of 1848

There are those who claim that the revolutionaries of 1848 created a myth by claiming Joseph II as their spiritual ancestor. The Emperor, they say, was an absolutist ruler who would have looked askance at anyone who demanded that the people govern themselves. Actually, what divided the democracy of the German left in 1848 from the absolutism of Joseph II were seventy years of historical development. In essence, if not in form, they had much in common. On the other hand, the adulation of Joseph II by the liberals was more than a romantic notion. By declaring themselves his heirs, the revolutionaries found a tradition, a degree of respectability, a link with the Austrian past. It is not unworthy of that tradition that one of their first moves was an attempt to bring about the final emancipation of the Austrian peasant.

To end labor services once and for all, Hans Kudlich, himself the son of a Silesian peasant, introduced a motion in the newly constituted Reichstag. It asked that " the Diet of the Empire resolve that, from this moment, hereditary subjection, and all rights and duties arising from it, be abolished." [30] " With it," he said in giving the justification for his bill, " the work which the Emperor Joseph had begun shall be concluded. What a monarch has done for his subjects we shall do for our brothers, for ourselves." [31]

More than half a century had passed since the death of Joseph II. Feudalism had, by violence or gradual agreement, been swept away in almost all European countries outside Austria, except Russia, and nobody in the revolutionary diet was willing to come to the defense of hereditary subjection *per se*. Yet the question as to whether labor services were a private agreement between lords and subjects, and their abolition therefore a breach of contract and injury to the rights of private property, haunted the left of the Reichstag as it had

30 H. Kudlich, *op. cit.*, II, 91.
31 *Ibid.*, II, 92.

haunted Joseph II. As a result the assembly lost itself in the most elaborate discussions on the origins of feudalism, and the legal nature of labor services and other obligations. Among those who thought themselves most competent to discuss the past as well as the present and future was the historian Alexander Helfert who thought that while the principle of abolition was a sound one, no actual liberation should take place until some method of indemnification had been agreed upon. He reasoned that the burghers and peasants in the Reichstag had no right to make provision about the property of the nobles, for these were not represented in it. The Reichstag, he said, was acting like the Holy Crispinus who took the leather from the rich to make shoes for the poor, and by this action would only arouse the poor proletariat of the village which had little to gain from the abolition of labor services (sic!). The night of August fourth, he called out to the assembly, ought to serve as a warning and not as an example. "He seems to have thought," Kudlich commented bitterly, "that the millions who had been sighing under the yoke of subjection for many centuries could wait a few days longer." [32]

They did not have to wait too long. On September 7, 1848, the law emancipating the Austrian peasantry was passed. It abolished all dues and services but guaranteed compensation to the owners. The law was not what the liberals had wanted. Yet it was a momentous event. The revolutionary diet had rid Austria of the last legal vestige of manorialism.

In the speech celebrating the event Kudlich once more paid tribute to the previous work of the Emperor Joseph:

No people have drunk deeper from the cup of serfdom than the Austrian people. And of all Austrians the peasant has been the most bitterly oppressed. There he lay in chains and could not move a limb. And beside him stood the cruel, greedy vultures who hacked his flesh and sucked his blood. So it was from year to year, from century to century. Fathers be-

32 *Ibid.*, II, 147-8.

queathed serfdom to their sons; the sons to grandsons. Many an eye looked to heaven with the reproach: Lord, when will this end?... The servitude has lasted long. Why? That misfortune steel us to be men. The good intentions of the Emperor Joseph—whom we remember in gratitude and reverence —were frustrated, that the people help themselves.[33]

Unfortunately Kudlich was wrong.[34] The peasantry did not come to the aid of the embattled democracy of 1848, the people did not " help themselves." Having attained its freedom, the peasantry decided that it was for law and order and stayed at home. The reform was completed, not by the representatives of the people, but by the victorious absolutism of Schwarzenberg, Stadion and Bach.

Yet this also was in character. In Joseph II, perhaps for the last time in Austrian history, liberalism and absolutism were one. After his death they parted, went their separate ways, became enemies. In 1848 they met again, enemies now, yet for an instant working for the same aim, the aim of peasant emancipation.

33 *Ibid.*, II, 209.

34 He paid for it by spending the rest of his life in exile. First in Switzerland and after 1854 as a doctor in Hoboken, N. J. He died in 1917 at the age of 94.

CONCLUSION

" BETWEEN 1500 and 1850," wrote Schmoller, " the problem of the peasantry was the great social question of the day." [1] For the countries which made up the Habsburg monarchy three dates within this period are of crucial importance: 1525-26, 1740-90 and 1848.

During the era of Maria Theresa and Joseph II the emancipation of the peasants in the German provinces of the Empire had none of the spectacular character of the agrarian reforms in the Slav provinces or in Hungary: the landowners were not as rich, the peasants not as poor, the chasm between the two was not as wide. Sharing in much of the legislation devised for Bohemia, Moravia and Silesia, the weakened feudal constitution of the German Austrian provinces could accept these measures more easily and assimilate them more successfully. On the other hand, the population of German Austria did not experience either, the gradual, eventless and on the whole peaceful dissolution of the status of subjection that took place in the provinces of Southern Germany. German Austria could boast of the whole range of feudal conditions in central Europe, from those in certain parts of Styria where, as Borié had exclaimed, conditions " were worse than in Hungary," to the free peasantry of Tyrol.

Tyrol was an exceptional case, however, and on the whole it could still be said of the Austrian peasant of the middle of the eighteenth century that he was a " helpless creature, poor through ignorance, frightened through poverty, mistreated through fear." By the end of the century he had become a human being; a human being whose freedom was restricted, whose self-determination was still hampered at every turn, but who had been shown the direction in which the realization of greater freedom lay. To have shown the way,

1 Gustav Schmoller, *Die Soziale Frage*, Munich, 1918, p. 558.

to have pointed out the direction was the achievement of Maria Theresa and Joseph II.

The beginnings had been humble and fumbling. Theoretically and practically they were lost in the all-pervading effort of securing money for the ever-growing needs of the state and the army. But action gave rise to thought. By the seventeen-seventies Maria Theresa's measures for the benefit of the peasantry were gradually assuming the character of a conscious reform program.

Nonetheless Maria Theresa had attempted to leave the existing social structure essentially unimpaired. And even if, under the influence of Blank, she sometimes spoke of abolishing " die Leibeigenschaft et les corvées " [2] (sic!), she was still not willing to do so except on her private estates, emphasizing again and again that she was introducing these changes not as a " sovereign ", but as a " manorial lord."

Maria Theresa, who was a kind woman, undoubtedly had a great deal of sympathy with the peasants, but this sympathy was necessarily limited by what she had come to consider the fundamental rights of the nobility. In the unphilosophical mind of the Empress who knew nothing of the " pre-established harmony " between the welfare of the society as a whole and that of every individual in it, there was a clear realization that every amelioration of peasant conditions, every reduction in dues, every curtailment of the lord's legal rights, would not only cause material losses for which, in spite of the reformers' assertions to the contrary, there could not in the long run be compensation, but would gradually render meaningless the status of nobility itself. And that, Maria Theresa, who felt that her and her son's succession had been saved by the Austro-Hungarian nobility, who had spent all her life among nobles, who herself was thoroughly imbued with the spirit and attitudes of aristocracy, could never have wished. " They were," wrote Gruenberg of the changes Maria Theresa

2 A. v. Arneth (ed.), *Briefe der Kaiserin Maria Theresia an ihre Kinder und Freunde*, 4 vols., Vienna, 1884, II, 66.

had introduced, " a piece of socio-political patchwork the aim of which was not the elimination of an intolerable condition, but on the contrary its retention." [3]

Maria Theresa's reforms may be patchwork to Gruenberg, as they had been patchwork to Joseph a century earlier. But the application of the term " patchwork " to these these reforms implies an ability to visualize a society basically different from a manorialism in which a mass of subjected peasants obeyed, respected, and served a privileged landowner. Gruenberg knew such a society, Joseph had conceived of one, Maria Theresa did neither.

And yet all the great reforms of Joseph II had their origins in the "patches" of Maria Theresa. Maria Theresa, not Joseph II, abolished the exemption of the nobles from taxation; she, not he, introduced the local governments as the protectors of the peasants in the province; she, not he, put the first serious limitations on the right of patrimonial justice. Even the most radical action of all, the abolition of labor services, was only an extension of Raab's System which had existed on the royal domains for many years.

Various conclusions can be drawn from these facts. One is that Maria Theresa deserves more credit for the emancipation of the Austrian peasant than she has generally been given. The writers of the *Vormärz* period and the revolution, for instance, hardly mention her at all, ascribing all that had been achieved to the " immortal Joseph " who at times is even specifically credited with measures introduced during his mother's reign, such as the *Robot* Patent of 1772.[4]

On the other hand, the reforms of Joseph II are also thrown into a different light. How could he, who carried on so conscientiously in the direction which Maria Theresa had shown him, be accused of violating historical continuity, of

3 K. Gruenberg, *Bauernbefreiung, op. cit.*, I, 276.

4 For instance, Heinrich Reschauer, *Das Jahr 1848*, Vienna, 1872, p. 30.

not understanding the needs of the people, of creating a general revolution?

It would be foolish to dismiss the legend of the " Revolutionary Emperor " altogether. Joseph II may have moved in the direction which his mother had indicated, but he moved with a different speed, in a different spirit. The aim of her endeavor seems to have been to manage as efficiently as possible under the existing state of affairs, leaving to her posterity a well-ordered, well-financed country, free from mass misery or subjection. Joseph II, on the other hand, was one of the few self-conscious reformers in a position of authority before the nineteenth century. That he was possessed of an intellectual vision of the equality of all before the state there can be little doubt. And only in terms of this vision, which he himself set up as measuring rod for his achievements, can he be pronounced a failure.

Why he did fail has been the subject of much discussion. The traditional reason that his work violated historical continuity no longer seems valid. The policy of equality and centralization was in a sense merely mercantilist practice carried to its logical conclusion. The methods which he used to achieve his ends were for the most part within the tradition of Austrian government, and while he is sometimes said to have been " unpopular " this is only true in that the one class of the population considered as " people," the nobility, was exactly the group which disliked him.

It has been suggested that his failure lay largely in his personality, tactlessness and harshness. But while it must be admitted that the Emperor was not exactly the soul of diplomacy, it can hardly be shown that he was more tactless than most other reformers. Peter the Great, with whom he has sometimes been compared in plans and intentions, was no paragon of tenderness either, and still succeeded where Joseph did not.

Perhaps the failure of the Emperor's plans lay in none of these things, but rather in circumstances over which he had little control and which were almost entirely unconnected with his reforms. When his social innovations were at their crucial stage, Austria went to war against Turkey. The fiasco of Joseph's campaign aroused the noble opposition which, although vociferous in its denunciation of his reforms, had hitherto remained inactive.

Even before the Eastern War, the Emperor's foreign policy was a continuous succession of disappointments. He was generally unpopular with foreign governments and aspersions were cast on everything he did, a situation which could not help but have an adverse effect upon the success of his domestic policies. To this unpopularity various factors may have contributed, but one stands out above all others: Joseph's nemesis, the Great Frederick, who, as Gottschalk has remarked, played " Mephistopheles to Joseph's Faust." [5] Joseph may not have been Faust but Frederick certainly was Mephisto, and even after he had died the seeds he had sown grew up to plague the Emperor.

Finally, at the moment when his whole system came to a crisis, the Emperor died. It may be rash to suggest that had he lived he could have mastered this crisis, but there is at least a possibility that he might have done so. Over his successors he had of course no control. But that the reign of Joseph II should be followed by that of Francis II and Metternich was a tragedy for the social progress of Austria for which the shortcomings of Joseph's methods can hardly be blamed.

The advent of the French Revolution curiously enough afforded comfort to both sides. In its early stages the opposition to the absolutism of the king in France encouraged the Austrian nobility until the fear of " liberty and equality " inspired a general reversion to conservatism, a trend which was again tempered by the apprehension that the peasants in turn might try to imitate the actions of their French *confrères*. And it

5 Louis Gottschalk, *The Era of the French Revolution*, Boston, 1929, p. 113.

was this apprehension which was finally instrumental in salvaging something of the Josephian reforms.

This remnant does not, by ordinary standards of measurement, confirm the legend of Joseph's complete failure. He had done a great deal more than any of his predecessors before 1740 and even with the achievements of Maria Theresa the net results of his work may be compared favorably. Economically and legally, he had, building on the foundations Maria Theresa had laid, constructed the framework within which the relations between landowners and peasants in Austria were to be confined for half a century. Together their work was a major part of what Schmoller has called " the greatest social reform in German history before the advent of social legislation in the second half of the nineteenth century." [6]

6 G. Schmoller, *op. cit.*, p. 581.

BIBLIOGRAPHY

LAWS AND OFFICIAL DOCUMENTS

Allgemeines Buergerliches Gesetzbuch. Vienna, 1786.
"Beilage No. 70," *Stenographische Protokolle des Hauses der Abgeordneten.* Vienna, 1886.
Broadsides: *Ausrottung der Spatzen wegen Schaedlichkeit fuer die Landwirtschaft* (March 1, 1762).
Avertissement (January 9, 1768).
Norma zur Häuserbeschreibung in Kärnten (August 7, 1758).
Stolordnung fuer die Hauptstadt Klagenfurt (August 16, 1762).
Handbuch aller unter der Regierung Kaiser Joseph II fuer die K. K. Erbländer Ergangenen Verordnungen und Gesetze. 18 vols., Vienna, 1785-1790.
Hauer, Ferdinand von. *Praktische Darstellung der in Oesterreich unter der Enns für das Unterthansfach Bestehenden Gesetze.* 3 vols., Vienna, 1824.
Historische Aktenstuecke ueber das Staendewesen in Oesterreich. Leipzig, 1847.
Sammlung aller fuer die K. K. Erblaender Ergangenen Gesetze und Verordnungen vom Jahre 1740-1780. 9 vols., Vienna, 1785.
Sammlung der Gesetze welche unter der Glorreichsten Regierung Koenig Leopold II in den Sämtlichen Erblanden Erschienen sind. 5 vols., Vienna, 1794-1796.

PERIODICALS AND ENCYCLOPEDIAS

Allgemeine Deutsche Bibliothek, Vol. XCIII. Berlin, 1790.
Czikam, J. J. and Graeffle, F. *Oesterreichische Nationalenzyclopedie.* Vienna, 1836.
Magazin fuer Geschichte, Statistik und Staatsrecht der Oesterreichischen Monarchie. Goettingen, 1806-1808.
Schloezer, August L. *Stats-Anzeigen.* 18 vols., Goettingen, 1780-1790.
Sonnenfels, Joseph von. "Der Mann ohne Vorurteil", *Gesammelte Schriften.* 10 vols., Vienna, 1783-1787.
Universallexikon aller Wissenschaften und Kuenste. 64 vols., Leipzig, 1732-1750.

SOCIAL AND ECONOMIC LITERATURE

Der Antiphysiocrat. Frankfurt, 1780.
Becher, Johann Joachim. *Politische Discurs.* Frankfurt, 1688.
——. *Psychosophia.* Hamburg, 1725.
Cramer, Johann. *Anleitung zum Forstwesen.* Braunschweig, 1766.
Florine, Philipp. *Adeliges Landleben.* Basel, 1748.
Der Frohndienst Abgeschafft ohne Prozess und Aufruhr. n. p., 1798.

191

Hassel, Georg. *Statistischer Abriss des Kaiserthums Oesterreich.* Nuremberg, 1807.

Herberts Versuche ueber die Allgemeine Kornpolizey. Vienna, 1790.

Hirzel, H. C. *Die Wirtschaft eines Philosophischen Bauers.* Zurich, 1774.

Hornick, P. W. von. *Oesterreich ueber Alles, wann es nur will.* Regensburg, 1727.

Justi, J. H. G. von. *Abhandlungen von der Macht, Glueckseligkeit und Credit eines Staates.* Ulm, 1787.

——. *Abhandlungen in den Oeconomischen und Cameralschriften.* Goettingen, 1755.

——. *Die Grundfeste zu der Macht und Glueckseligkeit der Staaten.* Koenigsberg, 1760.

——. *Grundriss einer Guten Regierung.* Frankfurt, 1759.

——. *Neue Wahrheiten zum Vorteil der Naturkunde und des Gesellschaftlichen Lebens der Menschen.* Leipzig, 1754.

——. *Oeconomische Schriften.* Berlin, 1760.

——. *Politische und Finanzschriften.* Kopenhagen, 1761.

——. *Staatswirtschaft.* 2 vols., Leipzig, 1758.

Klagen der Unterthanen der Oesterreichischen Monarchie wegen Aufhebung des Neuen Steuersystems und Wiedereinführung des Alten. n. p., 1790.

Die Kontribution. Vienna, 1788.

Kudler, Joseph. *Grundlehren der Volkswirtschaft.* Vienna, 1756.

Leibeigenschaft. n. p., n. d.

Mirabeau, Honoré de. *De la Monarchie Prussienne.* 7 vols., London, 1788.

Schroeder, Wilhelm von. *Fuerstliche Schatz- und Rentkammer.* Koenigsberg, 1752.

Simonde de Sismondi, J. C. L. de. *Nouveau Principes d'Economie Politique.* 2 vols., Paris, 1827.

Sonnenfels, Joseph von. "Die Erste Vorlesung in dem Akademischen Jahrgang, 1782", *Gesammelte Schriften.* 10 vols., Vienna, 1783-1788.

——. *Grundsaetze der Polizey, Handlung und Finanzwissenschaft.* Munich, 1787.

——. *Politische Abhandlungen.* Vienna, 1777.

POLITICAL PAMPHLETS

Andrian-Werburg, Viktor von. *Oesterreich und dessen Zukunft.* Hamburg, 1843.

Oesterreich im Jahre 1840. 2 vols., Leipzig, 1843.

Oesterreichs Innere Politik. Stuttgart, 1847.

Playfair, William, *Joseph and Benjamin, a Conversation.* London, 1787.

Schuselka, Franz. *Der Fortschritt und das Conservative Prinzip in Oesterreich.* Hamburg, 1847.

——. *Oesterreichische Vor- und Rueckschritte.* Leipzig, 1844.

——. *Oesterreich ueber Alles, wenn es nur will.* Hamburg, 1848.

Sealsfield, Charles. *Oesterreich wie es ist.* Vienna, 1919.

DESCRIPTION AND TRAVEL

Alexander, W. *Picturesque Representations of the Manners and of the Dress of the Austrians.* London, 1814.
Hoare, Sir Richard. *Recollections Abroad During the Years 1788, 1789, 1790.* Bath, 1814.
Montague, Lady Mary Wortley. *Letters from the Levant.* London, 1838.
Montesquieu, Charles de. *Voyages de Montesquieu.* Bordeaux, 1894-1896.
Nicolai, Friedrich. *Reise durch Deutschland.* 8 vols., Berlin, 1784-1788.
Richter, Joseph. *Eipeldauer Briefe.* Munich, 1917.
Serres, Marcel de. *Voyage dans l'Empire d'Autriche.* 4 vols., Paris, 1814.
Young, Arthur. *Travels in the Kingdom of France.* Dublin, 1793.

LETTERS AND MEMORANDA

Arneth, Alfred von (ed.). *Briefe der Kaiserin Maria Theresia an ihre Kinder und Freunde.* 4 vols., Vienna, 1884.
——, (ed.). "Denkschriften des Fuersten Kaunitz", *Archiv fuer Oesterreichische Geschichte.* Vienna, 1872.
——, (ed.) *Joseph II und Katherine von Russland, ihr Briefwechsel.* Vienna, 1869.
——, (ed.). *Joseph II und Leopold von Toskana, ihr Briefwechsel.* 2 vols., Vienna, 1782.
——, (ed.). *Maria Theresia und Joseph II, ihr Briefwechsel.* 3 vols., Vienna, 1867.
——, (ed.). "Zwei Denkschriften der Kaiserin Maria Theresia", *Archiv fuer Oesterreichische Geschichte.* Vienna, 1872.
Beer, Adolf (ed.). *Joseph II, Leopold II und Kaunitz, ihr Briefwechsel.* Vienna, 1872.
Botzenhart, Erich (ed.). *Freiherr vom Stein, Briefwechsel, Denkschriften, Aufzeichnungen.* 7 vols., Berlin, 1931.
Hartmann, Moritz. "Briefe aus dem Vormärz", *Bibliothek Deutscher Schriftsteller aus Boehmen.* Prag, 1911.
Rhyn, R. von. "Unveroeffentlichte Briefe der Kaiserin Maria Theresia", *Oesterreichische Rundschau.* Vienna, 1912.
Schloezer, August L. *Briefwechsel.* 9 vols., Goettingen, 1782-1792.
Wolf, Adam (ed.). "Ein Handbillet Kaiser Joseph II", *Beitraege zur Kunde Steiermärkischer Geschichtsquellen.* Graz, 1875.

MEMOIRS AND BIOGRAPHIES

Bauernfeld, Eduard. *Erinnerungen aus Alt-Wien.* Vienna, 1923.
Dohm, C. W. von. *Denkwuerdigkeiten aus meiner Zeit.* 3 vols., Lemgo, 1814.
Geissler, Adam F., Jr. "Erzaehlungen aus dem Charakter und Handlungen Joseph II", *Prophetische Mutmassungen ueber die Franzoesische Staatsveraenderung.* Philadelphia, 1794.
Helfert, J. A. "Erlebnisse und Erinnerungen", *Die Kultur.* Vienna, 1904.
Kudlich, Hans. *Rueckblicke und Erinnerungen.* 3 vols., Vienna, 1873.

194   BIBLIOGRAPHY

Kuebeck, Max von (ed.). *Die Tagebuecher des Karl Friedrich Freiherrn Kuebeck zu Kuebau.* 2 vols., Vienna, 1909.
Ligne, Charles J. Prince de. *Mémoires.* 5 vols., Paris, 1828.
Pettenegg, Gaston von (ed.). *Ludwig und Karl von Zinzendorf, ihre Selbstbiographien.* Vienna, 1879.
Pichler, Karoline. *Denkwuerdigkeiten aus meinem Leben.* 2 vols., Munich, 1914.
Redlich, Oswald. "Die Tagebuecher Karl VI", *Gesamtdeutsche Vergangenheit.* Munich, 1938.
Ségur, Louis Philippe de. *Mémoires.* 3 vols., Paris, 1824.
Sonnenfels, Joseph von. "Die Letzten Tage Theresiens", *Gesammelte Schriften.* 10 vols., Vienna, 1783-1787.

SECONDARY SOURCES

GENERAL WORKS

Beidtel, Ignaz. *Geschichte der Oesterreichischen Staatsverwaltung.* Innsbruck, 1889.
Biedermann, Karl. *Deutschland im Achtzehnten Jahrhundert.* 2 vols., Leipzig, 1880.
Bruegel, L. *Geschichte der Oesterreichischen Sozialdemokratie.* Vienna, 1922.
Bryce, James. *The Holy Roman Empire.* London, 1921.
Charmatz, Richard. *Oesterreichs Innere Geschichte.* Leipzig, 1918.
Dorn, Walter. *Competition for Empire.* New York, 1940.
Eger, Joseph. *Geschichte Tirols.* 4 vols., Innsbruck, 1880.
Friedjung, Heinrich. *Oesterreich von 1848 bis 1860.* Stuttgart, 1908.
Gershoy, Leo. *From Despotism to Revolution.* New York, 1944.
Goetz, W. (ed.). "Das Zeitalter des Absolutismus", *Propylaeen Weltgeschichte.* Berlin, 1931.
Gottschalk, Louis. *The Era of the French Revolution.* Boston, 1929.
Huber, Alfons. *Geschichte Oesterreichs.* 7 vols., Gotha, 1885-1938.
Jannssen, Johannes. *Geschichte des Deutschen Volkes.* Freiburg, 1897.
Kralik, Richard. *Oesterreichische Geschichte.* Vienna, 1914.
Krones, Franz. *Geschichte Oesterreichs.* 4 vols., Berlin, 1879.
Léger, Louis. *Histoire de l'Autriche-Hongrie.* Paris, 1920.
Mailath, János N. *Geschichte des Oesterreichischen Kaiserstaats.* Hamburg, 1850.
Marczali, Henry. *Hungary in the Eighteenth Century.* Cambridge, 1910.
Mayer, F. M. and Pirchegger, H. *Geschichte und Kulturleben Deutschoesterreichs.* Vienna, 1931.
Pirchegger, Hans. *Geschichte der Steiermark.* Gotha, 1920.
Pirenne, Henri. *Histoire de Belgique.* 7 vols., Brussels, 1907-1932.
Rudolf, Archduke of Austria, et al. (eds.). *Die Oesterreichische Monarchie in Wort und Bild.* Vienna, 1888.
Sassmann, Hans. *Das Reich der Träumer.* Berlin, 1932.
Springer, Anton. *Geschichte Oesterreichs seit dem Wiener Frieden.* 2 vols., Leipzig, 1863.

Uhlirz, Karl. *Handbuch der Geschichte Oesterreichs und seiner Nachbar-laender Ungarn und Boehmen.* 2 vols., Graz, 1927.

Valsecchi, Franco. *L'Assolutismo Illuminato in Austria e in Lombardia.* Bologna, 1931.

Werthheimer, E. *Geschichte Oesterreichs und Ungarns im Ersten Jahrzehnt des Neunzehnten Jahrhunderts.* Leipzig, 1884-1890.

Wolf, Adam and Zwiedineck-Suedenhorst, Hans von. *Oesterreich unter Maria Theresia, Joseph II und Leopold II.* Berlin, 1884.

BIOGRAPHIES OR BIOGRAPHICAL ARTICLES

Andreas, Willy. "Maria Theresia", in *Die Grossen Deutschen.* Berlin, 1937.

Arneth, Alfred von. "Johann Christoph Bartenstein", *Archiv fuer Oester-reichische Geschichte.* Vienna, 1871.

——. *Geschichte Maria Theresias.* 10 vols., Vienna, 1863-1879.

Beer, Adolf. "Die Zusammenkuenfte Joseph II und Friedrich II zu Neisse und Neustadt", *Archiv fuer Oesterreichische Geschichte.* Vienna, 1895.

Benedikt, Ernst. *Kaiser Joseph II.* Vienna, 1936.

Bibl, Viktor. *Kaiser Franz.* Leipzig, 1938.

——. *Kaiser Franz und sein Erbe.* Vienna, 1922.

——. *Kaiser Joseph II.* Vienna, 1943.

Bright, J. F. *Joseph II.* London, 1905.

Charmatz, Richard. *Adolf Fischhof.* Stuttgart, 1910.

Engel-Jánosi, Friedrich. "Joseph II Tod im Urteil der Zeitgenossen", *Oesterreichisches Institut fuer Geschichtsforschung.* Innsbruck, 1930.

Fournier, August. "Joseph II", *Historische Skizzen und Studien.* Prag, 1885.

Gerstenberg, Heinrich. "Philipp Wilhelm von Hornick", *Jahrbuecher fuer Nationaloekonomie und Statistik.* Jena, 1930.

Gruenberg, Karl. "Franz Anton von Blank", *Schmollers Jahrbuch fuer Gesetzgebung, Verwaltung und Volkswirtschaft im Deutschen Reich.* Munich, 1911.

Guglia, Eugen. *Maria Theresia.* 2 vols., Munich, 1917.

Herr, Ottfried. *Johann Joachim Becher.* Limburg, 1936.

Ilwof, Franz. *Die Grafen von Attems.* Graz, 1897.

——. "Kaiser Joseph II als Volkswirt", *Preussische Jahrbuecher.* Berlin, 1907.

Kauder, Emil. "Johann Joachim Becher", *Schmollers Jahrbuch fuer Gesetzgebung, Verwaltung und Volkswirtschaft im Deutschen Reich.* Munich, 1924.

Kern, Theodor von. "Die Reformen Maria Theresias", *Historisches Taschenbuch.* Leipzig, 1869.

Kretschmayr, Heinrich. "Joseph II", *Velhagen und Klasings Monatshefte.* Berlin, 1927.

——. *Maria Theresia.* Leipzig, 1938.

Langsam, Walter C. "Emperor Francis and the Austrian Jacobins", *American Historical Review.* Richmond, 1945.

Lupas, Ioan. "L'Empereur Joseph II et Horia", *Revue de Transylvanie.* Cluj, 1935.

196 BIBLIOGRAPHY

Lustkandl, W. *Sonnenfels und Kudler.* Vienna, 1891.
Mitrofanov, P. P. *Joseph II.* Vienna, 1910.
Mueller, Willibald. *Joseph von Sonnenfels.* Vienna, 1882.
Padover, Saul. *The Revolutionary Emperor.* London, 1934.
Paganel, Camille. *Histoire de Joseph II.* Paris, 1845.
Remer, Justus. *Johann Heinrich Gottlieb von Justi.* Stuttgart, 1938.
Rizzi, H. "Johann Joachim Becher", *Die Kultur.* Vienna, 1904.
Srbik, Heinrich von. *Metternich, der Staatsmann und Mensch.* 2 vols., Munich, 1925.
——. "Wilhelm von Schroeder", *Kaiserliche Akademie der Wissenschaften, Sitzungsberichte.* Vienna, 1910.
Walter, Joseph. *Joseph II.* Budweis, 1913.
Wendrinsky, Johann. *Kaiser Joseph II.* Vienna, 1880.
Wiedemann-Warnheim, Adolf von. "Joseph II", *Historisches Jahrbuch.* Munich, 1915.
Wolf, Adam. "Graf Rudolf Chotek", *Kaiserliche Akademie der Wissenschaften, Sitzungsberichte.* Vienna, 1853.
——. "Graf Karl Zinzendorf", *Geschichtliche Bilder aus Oesterreich.* Vienna, 1878.

SPECIAL PERIODS

1525-1526

Bax, E. Belfort. *The Peasants' War in Germany.* London, 1899.
Bebel, August. *Der Deutsche Bauernkrieg.* Braunschweig, 1876.
Engels, Friedrich. *Der Deutsche Bauernkrieg.* Berlin, 1908.
Franz, Guenther. *Der Deutsche Bauernkrieg.* Berlin, 1933.
Honold, Walter. *Die Meraner Artikel.* Tuebingen, 1936.

1526-1626

Czerny, Albin. *Bilder aus der Zeit der Bauernunruhen.* Linz, 1876.
——. *Der Zweite Bauernaufstand in Oberoesterreich.* Linz, 1890.

1753-64

Guba, A. "Steiermark waehrend des Siebenjaehrigen Krieges", *Historischer Verein fuer Steiermark.* Graz, 1902-1903.

1848

Bach, Maximilian. *Geschichte der Wiener Revolution,* Vienna, 1898.
Engel-Jánosi, Friedrich. "Kaiser Joseph II in der Wiener Bewegung des Jahres 1848", *Mitteilungen des Vereines fuer Geschichte der Stadt Wien.* Vienna, 1931.
Friedjung, Heinrich. "Freunde und Gegner der Bauernbefreiung in Oesterreich", *Historische Aufsaetze.* Stuttgart, 1919.
Helfert, J. A. *Geschichte der Wiener Revolution.* 7 vols., Freiburg, 1907-1909.
Reschauer, Heinrich. *Das Jahr 1848.* Vienna, 1872.

Srbik, Heinrich von. "Die Wiener Revolution des Jahres 1848 in Sozial-geschichtlicher Beleuchtung", *Schmollers Jahrbuch fuer Gesetzgebung, Verwaltung und Volkswirtschaft im Deutschen Reich.* Munich, 1919.

Stiles, W. H. *Austria in 1848-49.* New York, 1852.

Zenker, E. V. *Die Wiener Revolution.* Vienna, 1897

SOCIAL AND ECONOMIC BACKGROUND

Adler, Max. *Die Anfaenge der Merkantilistischen Gewerbepolitik in Oester-reich.* Vienna, 1903.

Bauer-Mengelberg, Kaethe. *Agrarpolitik.* Leipzig, 1931.

Beer, Adolf. "Staatsschulden und die Ordnung des Staatshaushaltes unter Maria Theresia", *Archiv fuer Oesterreichische Geschichte.* Vienna, 1895.

Beidtel, Ignaz. "Zur Geschichte der Feudalverfassung in den Deutschen Provinzen der Oesterreichischen Monarchie unter der Regierung der Kaiserin Maria Theresia", *Kaiserliche Akademie der Wissenschaften, Sitzungsberichte.* Vienna, 1853.

——. "Zur Geschichte der Feudalverfassung in den Deutschen Provinzen der Oesterreichischen Monarchie unter der Regierung Kaiser Joseph II", *Kaiserliche Akademie der Wissenschaften, Sitzungsberichte.* Vienna, 1853.

——. "Zur Geschichte der Feudalverfassung in den Deutschen Provinzen der Oesterreichischen Monarchie unter der Regierung Kaiser Leopold II", *Kaiserliche Akademie der Wissenschaften, Sitzungsberichte.* Vienna, 1853.

Bibl, Viktor. "Das Robot-Provisorium fuer Niederoesterreich", *Jahrbuch fuer Landeskunde Niederoesterreichs.* Vienna, 1905.

Brownlow, R. W. *Slavery and Serfdom in Europe.* London, 1892.

Buchenberger, A. *Agrarwesen und Agrargeschichte.* 2 vols., Leipzig, 1892.

Cronbach, Else. "Das Landwirtschaftliche Betriebsproblem", *Studien zur Sozial-, Wirtschafts- und Verwaltungsgeschichte.* Vienna, 1907.

Dopsch, Alfons. "Die Aeltere Wirtschafts- und Sozialgeschichte der Bauern in den Alpenlaendern Oesterreichs", *Instituttet for Sammenlignende Kulturforskning.* Oslo, 1930.

Engel-Jánosi, Friedrich. "Ueber die Entwicklung der Sozialen und Staats-wirtschaftlichen Verhaeltnisse im Deutschen Oesterreich, 1815-1848", *Vierteljahresschrift fuer Sozial- und Wirtschaftsgeschichte.* Berlin, 1924.

Gehlert, J. V. "Die Ergebnisse der in Oesterreich im vorigen Jahrhundert Ausgefuehrten Volkszaehlungen", *Kaiserliche Akademie der Wissen-schaften, Sitzungsberichte.* Vienna, 1855.

Grossmann, Henryk. "Oesterreichische Handelspolitik", *Studien zur Sozial-, Wirtschafts- und Verwaltungsgeschichte,* Vienna, 1914.

Goltz, Theodor von der. *Geschichte der Deutschen Landwirtschaft.* Stutt-gart, 1902.

Gruenberg, Karl. *Die Bauernbefreiung...in Boehmen, Maehren und Schlesien.* Leipzig, 1894.

——. *Studien zur Oesterreichischen Agrargeschichte.* Leipzig, 1901.

Heckscher, Eli F. *Mercantilism.* 2 vols., Mendel Shapiro trans., London, 1935.

Knapp, Georg F. "Leibeigenschaft in Oesterreich", *Beilage zur Allgemeinen Zeitung.* Munich, 1892.

Kraus, V. F. von. *Die Wirtschafts- und Verwaltungspolitik des Aufgeklaerten Absolutismus.* Freiburg, 1899.

Leimdoerfer, Max. "Brandschadenversicherung in Oesterreich", *Studien zur Sozial-, Wirtschafts- und Verwaltungsgeschichte.* Vienna, 1905.

Macartnay, C. A. *The Social Revolution in Austria.* Cambridge, 1926.

Mell, Anton. *Die Anfaenge der Bauernbefreiung im Steiermark.* Graz, 1901.

Mensi, Franz. "Die Geschichte der Direkten Steuern im Steiermark", *Forschungen zur Verfassungs- und Verwaltungsgeschichte der Steiermark.* Graz, 1910.

Mises, Ludwig von. "Die Entwicklung des Gutsherrlichen-Bäuerlichen Verhaeltnisses in Galizien", *Wiener Staatswissenschaftliche Studien.* Vienna, 1902.

Otto, Archduke of Austria. *Coutumes et Droits Successoraux de la Classe Paysanne et l'Indivision des Proprietées Rurales en Autriche.* Vienna, 1935.

Preser, Karl. *Die Erhaltung des Bauernstandes.* Leipzig, 1894.

Pribram, Alfred F. (ed.). *Materialien zur Geschichte der Preise und Loehne in Oesterreich.* Vienna, 1938.

Roscher, Wilhelm. *Die Nationaloekonomik des Ackerbaus.* Stuttgart, 1875.

——. "Oesterreichische Nationaloekonomik unter Leopold I", *Jahrbuecher fuer Nationaloekonomik und Statistik.* Jena, 1846.

——. "Der Saechsische Nationaloekonom Johann Heinrich Gottlieb von Justi", *Archiv fuer Saechsische Geschichte.* Leipzig, 1868.

——. *System der Volkswirtschaft.* Stuttgart, 1882.

——. "Zwei Saechsische Staatswirte", *Archiv fuer Saechsische Geschichte.* Leipzig, 1863.

Schmoller, Gustav. *The Mercantile System in Its Historical Significance.* New York, 1896.

——. *Die Soziale Frage.* Munich, 1918.

Schuenemann, K. "Oesterreichische Bevoelkerungspolitik unter Maria Theresia", *Deutsche Rundschau.* Berlin, 1935.

——. "Die Wirtschaftspolitik Joseph II in der Zeit seiner Mitregentschaft", *Oesterreichisches Institut fuer Geschichtsforschung, Mitteilungen.* Innsbruck, 1933.

Small, Albion. *The Cameralists.* Chicago, 1910.

Seton-Watson, R. W. "Metternich and Internal Austrian Policy", *Slavonic and East European Review.* London, 1939.

Sombart, Werner. *Der Moderne Kapitalismus.* 3 vols., Munich, 1921.

Sommer, Louise. "Die Oesterreichischen Kameralisten", *Studien zur Sozial-, Wirtschafts- und Verwaltungsgeschichte.* Vienna, 1920.

Suggenheim, Samuel. *Geschichte der Aufhebung der Leibeigenschaft.* St. Petersburg, 1861.

Zielenzinger, Kurt. "Die Alten Deutschen Kameralisten", *Beitraege zur Geschichte der Nationaloekonomie*. Jena, 1914.

Zwiedineck-Suedenhorst, Hans von. *Dorfleben im Achtzehnten Jahrhundert.*

ADMINISTRATIVE AND LEGAL BACKGROUND

Bibl, Viktor. "Die Niederoesterreichischen Staende und die Franzoesische Revolution", *Jahrbuch fuer Landeskunde Niederoesterreichs*, Vienna, 1905.

Bidermann, H. J. "Die Verfassungskrisis im Steiermark", *Mitteilungen des Historischen Vereines fuer Steiermark.* Graz, 1873.

Hintze, Otto. "Der Oesterreichische Beamtenstaat im Siebzehnten und Achzehnten Jahrhundert", *Historische Zeitschrift.* Munich, 1901.

Hock, K. von and Bidermann, H. J. *Der Oesterreichische Staatsrath.* Vienna, 1879.

Huber, Alfons. *Oesterreichische Reichsgeschichte.* Vienna, 1901.

Ilwof, Franz. "Der Staendische Landtag des Herzogthums Steiermark unter Maria Theresia und ihren Soehnen", *Archiv fuer Oesterreichische Geschichte.* Vienna, 1914.

Kern, Fritz. "Vom Herrenstaat zum Wohlfahrtsstaat", *Schmollers Jahrbuch fuer Gesetzgebung, Verwaltung und Volkswirtschaft im Deutschen Reich.* Munich, 1928.

Luschin von Ebengreuth, Arnold von. *Grundriss der Oesterreichischen Reichsgeschichte.* Bamberg, 1889.

Stolz, Otto. "Geschichte der Gerichte Deutschtirols", *Archiv fuer Oesterreichische Geschichte.* Vienna, 1913.

INTELLECTUAL BACKGROUND

Becker, Carl. *The Heavenly City of the Eighteenth Century Philosophers.* New Haven, 1932.

Bucher, W. *Grillparzers Verhaeltniss zu der Politik seiner Zeit.* Marburg, 1913.

Cassirer, Ernst. *Die Philosophie der Aufklaerung.* Tuebingen, 1932.

Klassens, Peter. *Die Grundlagen des Aufgeklaerten Absolutismus.* Jena, 1929.

Meyer, Christian. *Oesterreich und die Aufklaerung des Achtzehnten Jahrhunderts.* Hamburg, 1896.

Menzel, Adolf. "Ein Oesterreichischer Staatsphilosoph des Achtzehnten Jahrhunderts", *Oesterreichische Rundschau.* Vienna, 1905.

Richter, H. M. *Geistesstroemungen.* Berlin, 1875.

Srbik, Heinrich von. "Der Ideengehalt des Metternichschen Systems", *Historische Zeitschrift.* Munich, 1925.

Voltelini, Hans von. "Die Naturrechtlichen Lehren und die Reformen des Achtzehnten Jahrhunderts", *Historische Zeitschrift.* Munich, 1910.

INDEX

Administration, 43-46, 115-118, 163-165
Agricultural Revolution, 85
Agricultural Societies, 87
Andrian-Werburg, Viktor von, 174-175
Arneth, Alfred von, 34
Austerlitz, Battle of, 171

Bach, Alexander, 184
Ball, John, 11
Bankruptcy, state, of 1811, 172
Bannleihe, 18
Barefeet, 11
Bauernfeld, Eduard, 180-181
Becher, Johann Joachim, 23, 27-30
Beidtel, Ignaz, 70
Belgium, 146
Besthaupt, 17
Bielitz, 48
Blank, Franz Anton von, 48, 186
Bohemia, 34, 36, 56, 105-109, 111, 185
Breteuil, Baron Louis-Auguste, 113

Cameralism, 23-31, 92, 111
Carinthia, 15, 17, 37, 61, 65, 83, 109, 128, 151, Estates of, 38, 43, 141
Carniola, 17, 37, 109, 151, Estates of 43, 141
Catherine II, Empress of Russia, 89
Census, 69
Chancellery, Austro-Bohemian, 55, 59, 124, 131, 135, 138-39
Charles V, Emperor of the Holy Roman Empire, 96
Charles VI, Emperor of the Holy Roman Empire, 19-20, 35
Charles VII, Emperor of the Holy Roman Empire, 34
Chotek, Count Rudolf, 139, 164-165
Christina, Duchess of Saxe-Teschen, 96
Cilli, 59
Code of Civil Law (*Allgemeines Buergerliches Gesetzbuch*), 159
Colbert, Jean Baptiste, 91, 94
Common pasture, division of, 66-67
Communtation of dues and services, 51, 104, 129-131, 140-141, 156, 165-168, 173-174, 176-177, 180
Conscription, 69
Council of State, 42, 91, 126, 139
Court Conference, 164

Crispinus, St., 183
Croquants, 11
Curti, *Referent* von, 58

Decennalrecess, 35-37
Diedrichstein, possessions, 14
Diggers, 27
Directorium in publicis et camera-libus, 42
Documentary tax, 166
Domestic land, 15, 128
Domestic servants, 109-110
Dopsch, Alfons, 16

Education, rural, 74-76
Eger, Friedrich, 131, 138, 166-167, 176
Encyclopedists, 90
Enlightenment, 89-90, 92-93
Entail, 126
Eviction, 104, 123-126, 130, 165

"Fallen women", 111-112
Favorita, 19
Fee on departure (*Abfahrtsgeld*), 63, 109-111, 163
Ferdinand II, Emperor of the Holy Roman Empire, 24
Fire protection, 82-84, 144
Francis II, Emperor of the Holy Roman Empire (Francis I, Emperor of Austria), 160-161, 164, 166, 168-170, 173, 176-177, 179-180, 189
Frederick II, King of Prussia, 31, 89-90, 95, 189
Freistiftlichkeit, 65
French Revolution of 1789, 146, 155-156, 165, 168-169, 189
Friedjung, Heinrich, 165
Froidevaux, Joseph Hyazint von, 126
Fuerst, Chancellor von, 42

Galicia, 63, 111, 173, Estates of, 141
Gebler, Tobias von, 32, 132
Geisslern, Johann Georg von, 168
German Order, 19
Gottschalk, Louis, 189
Graz, 59
Greiner, Franz von, 42
Grillparzer, Franz, 180-181
Grossmann, Henryk, 156

201

202INDEX

Gruen, Anastasius (Anton Alexander Count Auersperg), 180-181
Gruenberg, Karl, 22-23, 186-187
Guglia, Eugen, 38

Hartmann, Moritz, 180
Hassels, Georg, 122
Hatzfeld, Count Karl Friedrich, 166
Haugwitz, Count Friedrich Wilhelm, 35-36, 42
Headman of village (Dorfrichter), 20
Heckscher, Eli F., 23
Helfert, Joseph Alexander, 183
Henry IV, King of France, 94
Herberstein, Count Ernst, 53
Herberstein, Count Leopold, 59
High Court of Justice, 42
Hoare, Sir Richard, 171
Holger, Ritter von, 179
Homer, 99
Hornick, Philipp Wilhelm von, 24-26, 92
Hungary, 16, 47, 105, 111, 146, 185, Estates of, 141
Hunting rights, 84-85, 145-146

Illegitimacy, 112
Inner Austria, 37, 43, 117, 128
Innleute, 50, 60, 63, 130

Joseph II, Emperor of the Holy Roman Empire, 12-13, 15-16, 22-23, 30, 32, 36-37, 40, 56-57, 61, 63, 88-98, 103, 105-151, 153-172, 174-179, 181-190
Judenburg, 58
Justi, Johann Heinrich Gottlieb, 20, 32, 66, 79, 80-81, 85, 92-93, 98, 102-103, 105, 123, 131
Justice, 46-47, 118-122, 162

Kaunitz-Rittberg, Prince Wenzel Anton, n63, 74-76, 148
Kees, Franz Georg von, 126, 161, 164, 166
Khevenhueller, Count Johann Franz, 117
Knapp, Georg Friedrich, 22-23
Kolowrat, Count Leopold, 135, 166, 168, 174
Kolowrat, Count Franz A., 180
Kremsmuenster, 82
Kudlich, Hans, 179, 182-184
Kuebeck zu Kuebau, Karl Friedrich von, 178-180

Labor services, 16-17, 48-61, 129-131, 140, 142, 165-168, 172-173, 175-177, 180, 182-184, 187
Laibach, Bishop of, 18
Landholding, 14-16, 64-68, 122-129, 158-159
Laudemium, 17, 62
Laudemium minor, 61
Lavant, Bishop of, 18
Law Concerning Subjects of 1781 (Untertanspatent), 119-120, 148, 162
Legungen, 64
Leimdoerfer, Ernst, 82-83
Lenau, Nicolaus, 180
Leopold I, Emperor of the Holy Roman Empire, 17, 24
Leopold II, Emperor of the Holy Roman Empire, 32, 143, 148-151, 157-160, 162-163, 165-166, 177-178
Lessing, Gotthold Ephraim, 181
Letter of release (Losbrief), 63
Levellers, 27
Lists of conduct (Konduitenlisten), 115-116
Local government (Kreisamt), 43-45, 114-115, 117, 163, 187
Locella, Ernst von, 48
Lower Austria, 17-18, 37, 43, 48-49, 52-55, 83, 110, 166, Estates of, 36, 48, 141, 148-149, 158, 163, 173-174

Manorial dues, 17, 61-64
Marburg, 59
Maria Theresa, Empress of the Holy Roman Empire, 12-13, 17, 19, 31-38, 40-42, 44-46, 48, 52, 55-56, 58-59, 61-2, 64, 68, 70, 73-74, 79, 83-84, 87-88, 95, 100, 114, 117, 119, 124, 144, 152-153, 163, 169-170, 175-178, 185-188, 190
Martini, Karl Anton von, 32-33, 92
Matthias, Archduke of Austria, 13
Mell, Anton, 53
Mercy-Argenteau, Count Florimund, 56
Metternich, Prince Clement Lothar, 160, 168, 178, 180, 189
Metternich System, 153, 180-181
Mirabeau, Count Gabriel Honoré Riquetti, 91-92, 113, 121
Mitrofanov, Pavel P., 112
Montague, Lady Mary Wortley, n19
Montesquieu, Baron Charles Louis de Secondat de, 90, 92
Moravia, 36, 56, 105-106, 108, 185
Mortuarium, 17, 61-62, 150
Muenzer, Thomas, 11